HTML

Visual Quic [barcode] e

rf

HTML Visual Quick Reference

Library of Congress Catalog No.: 95-069583

ISBN: 0-7897-0411-0

98 97 96 95   6 5 4 3 2 1

Interpretation of the printing code: the rightmost double-digit number is the year of the book's printing; the rightmost single-digit number, the number of the book's printing. For example, a printing code of 95-1 shows that the first printing of the book occurred in 1995.

Publisher Roland Elgey

Associate Publisher Stacy Hiquet

Publishing Director Brad R. Koch

Managing Editor Sandy Doell

Director of Marketing Lynn E. Zingraf

Acquisitions Editor
Beverly M. Eppink

Product Director
Jim Minatel

Production Editor
Heather Kaufman Urschel

Technical Editor
Warren Ernst
Alfonso Hermida

Figure Specialist
Cari Skaggs

Book Designer
Kim Scott

Cover Designer
Ruth Harvey

Acquisitions Assistant
Ruth Slates

Operations Coordinator
Patty Brooks

Editorial Assistant
Andrea Duvall

Production Team
Claudia Bell, Amy Cornwell, Anne Dickerson,
DiMonique Ford, John Hulse, Beth Lewis,
Clair Schweinler, Michael Thomas, Scott Tullis

Indexer
Rebecca Mayfield

Composed in *Stone Serif* and *Helvetica* by Que Corporation

About the Author

Dean Scharf is a creative director. He directs and supervises all phases of a project from concept to implementation. Recent projects have included books (*The Wall Street Journal* guides), interactive information kiosks, multimedia CD-ROMs, and online interfaces.

Dean Scharf has worked in the fields of Interactive Media, Advertising, Corporate Identity, and Simplified Communications. He has more than 20 years experience in design, production, planning, scheduling, execution, and delivery of print, artwork, and photography. Mr. Scharf has converted traditional design studios into state-of-the-art desktop publishing facilities.

Dean Scharf has worked in a variety of design firms and corporate design departments, including Lightbulb Press, Siegel & Gale, CBS Records, Clairol, Chermayeff and Geismar, and Donovan and Green.

Dean Scharf studied art history and architecture at Columbia University in New York City. He continues to paint and exhibit his artwork.

Acknowledgments

I would like to thank

Beverly for liking the idea,

Brad and others for saying yes to it,

Jim for the Windows pages and making sure I know what I'm writing about,

Warren for the UNIX pages,

Heather for making me look like I know how to spell and punctuate,

Design and Production for getting this book to press,

Krista for listening to me rant and rave,

Aroma for her patience, and

Timber for distracting me.

Trademarks

Contents

Part III Forms

Part IV Designing HTML Documents

Part V Posting Pages

Part VI Getting Your Files Noticed

Part VII Appendix

Preface

Once upon a time not too long ago, I was trying to find information about something new called HTML. I knew it was a programming language for publishing documents on the World Wide Web, a graphical part of the Internet. And I knew I had to learn Web programming to keep up with the changes in the publishing industry.

I asked around and found a few facts. First, I found out that there wasn't a good book available. Perhaps you had the same experience. Surfing the Web for documentation. Scouring bookstore shelves for a simple HTML book.

Eventually, I found what I needed on the Web and on bookstore shelves. However, what I found was not clear or concise. I could see that HTML programming was easy to understand but that the documentation wasn't. I just wanted to know what code to type and how to use it. What are the limitations? How do I specify type, control graphic design, insert images, and link files? And, I wanted it in a book that was easy to use.

So I found the simple answers and put them in this book.

Each set of facing pages presents one topic. I include some information on posting pages, where to find servers, how to structure documents, and a few design tips, but the bulk of the book focuses on the code. You can go pretty far on the basics because there isn't much more to HTML programming than the basics.

This book is for anyone who wants to get started with HTML and for people who want a quick reference at their side. You don't need a week to learn HTML basics. Just an hour, this book, a word processor, and a browser will do.

Buy this book if you want to:

- understand how Web pages are created
- find the simple facts about Web programming
- create Web pages of your own
- have a quick reference to check as you program
- learn more programming techniques
- make the transition from desktop publishing to online publishing
- establish a presence on the Internet for your business

- get informed before hiring an Internet programmer
- spend less than what other books cost

If you want a deeper understanding of HTML programming and the World Wide Web after you read this book, Que has published several related books that should be of interest:

Special Edition Using HTML

Special Edition Using the World Wide Web with Mosaic

Special Edition Using the Internet, Second Edition

Running a Perfect Web Site

All these books should be available at your local bookstore. You can also find information about these and other Que books on the Web at **http://www.mcp.com**, the Macmillan Information SuperLibrary.

Dean Scharf

What Is HTML?

HTML is a mark-up, or formatting, language. In fact, *HTML* stands for *HyperText Markup Language*. You mark up text files with HTML tags so that they can be read over a network or locally on your computer by browsing software. *Tags* are pieces of code surrounded by the symbols **<** and **>**. Browsers read tags when formatting HTML files on your screen. Documents available on the World Wide Web are HTML files.

HTML does not describe a page the way some computer languages do. Some languages actually describe every graphic element and its position on the page. This includes fonts, point sizes, screen values, line weights, and so on. In contrast, HTML describes neither text or graphic elements nor their placement. HTML only *tags* the content of the file with certain attributes that are later defined by the browser used to view the file. It is like a person who writes a memo by hand and puts small comments before certain sections of the memo to indicate to the secretary specific things to do, i.e., "new paragraph here," "new page," "please highlight this sentence," and so on.

HTML tags attribute type styles, insert graphics, sound, and video files in the text, and create hypertext links and forms. *Hypertext* is the most important capability of the HTML language. It means that any piece of text or graphic can link to another HTML document.

The official HTML language is a specific set of tags that all browsers should interpret. Some browsers are capable of interpreting additional tags outside the standard. New tags are added to the standard set over time.

Mosaic, a commonly used browser, was developed by the National Center for Supercomputing Applications (NSCA) at the University of Illinois. It combined color graphics with HTML text capabilities for the first time. These days Netscape, developed by people formerly at NSCA, is becoming the browser of choice because of its speed and enhanced features. One internet access provider I know requires you to use the Web browser they developed.

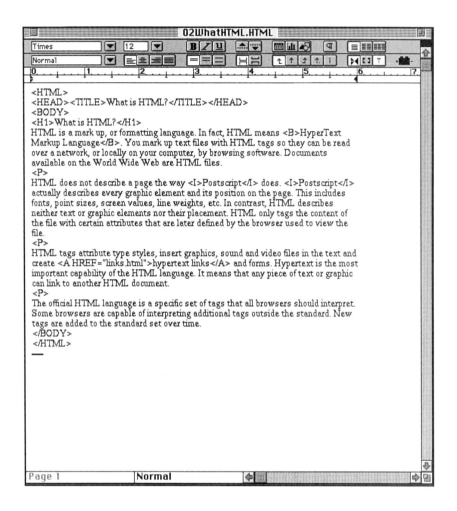

```
<HTML>
<HEAD><TITLE>What is HTML?</TITLE></HEAD>
<BODY>
<H1>What is HTML?</H1>
HTML is a mark up, or formatting language. In fact, HTML means <B>HyperText
Markup Language</B>. You mark up text files with HTML tags so they can be read
over a network, or locally on your computer, by browsing software. Documents
available on the World Wide Web are HTML files.
<P>
HTML does not describe a page the way <I>Postscript</I> does. <I>Postscript</I>
actually describes every graphic element and its position on the page. This includes
fonts, point sizes, screen values, line weights, etc. In contrast, HTML describes
neither text or graphic elements nor their placement. HTML only tags the content of
the file with certain attributes that are later defined by the browser used to view the
file.
<P>
HTML tags attribute type styles, insert graphics, sound and video files in the text and
create <A HREF="links.html">hypertext links</A> and forms. Hypertext is the most
important capability of the HTML language. It means that any piece of text or graphic
can link to another HTML document.
<P>
The official HTML language is a specific set of tags that all browsers should interpret.
Some browsers are capable of interpreting additional tags outside the standard. New
tags are added to the standard set over time.
</BODY>
</HTML>
```

Page 1   Normal

How HTML Works on the Web

Like e-mail, FTP, Gopher, and other Internet services, the World Wide Web requires an interconnected complex of hardware running specialized software to work on the Internet.

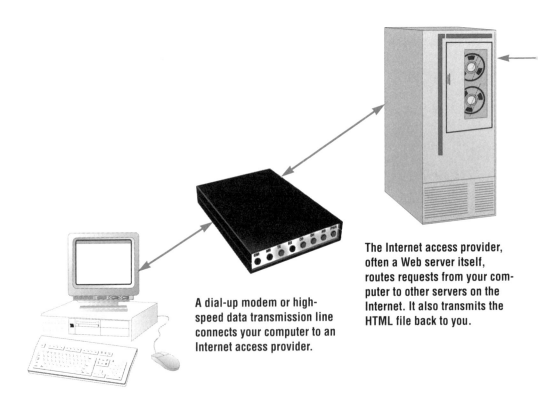

The Internet access provider, often a Web server itself, routes requests from your computer to other servers on the Internet. It also transmits the HTML file back to you.

A dial-up modem or high-speed data transmission line connects your computer to an Internet access provider.

The browser on your computer sends requests for HTML files to remote servers on the Internet by using addresses called *URLs* (Uniform Resource Locators). When the data returns to your computer, the browser interprets the HTML tags and displays the formatted text along with any graphics.

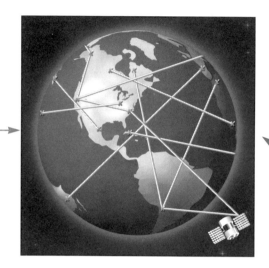

The Internet is a worldwide network of servers. Your request bounces from server to server until the URL address of the HTML file you want is found. The data then returns over the Internet to your computer.

The Web server holds the HTML file you are looking for along with any other files needed by the file, including graphic, sound, and video files inserted in it, and associated programs known as gateway scripts. *Gateway scripts* are programs running on the server that process data.

How Browsers Work

Browsers send requests and receive the data needed to display the HTML page on your screen. This includes the HTML file itself plus all the graphic, sound, and video files mentioned in it. Once the data is retrieved, the browser formats the type as indicated by the HTML tags and displays it with the graphics files on your computer screen.

When you click on a hypertext link, a new request to retrieve another file is sent out over the Internet. Some browsers perform other functions, such as sending e-mail or downloading files via FTP. *Helper applications* on your computer enable the browser to play sound and video inserted in the HTML file.

The fonts installed on your computer and the display preferences in the browser you use determine how text is formatted.

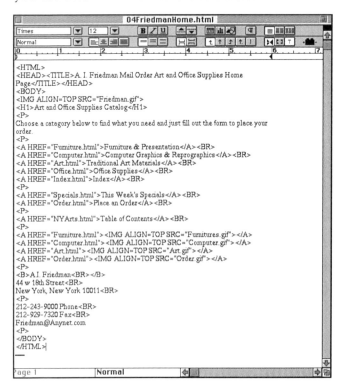

HTML files look like a mix of text and coding when viewed in a word processing program. The code is comprised of symbols and acronyms interspersed with text and file titles.

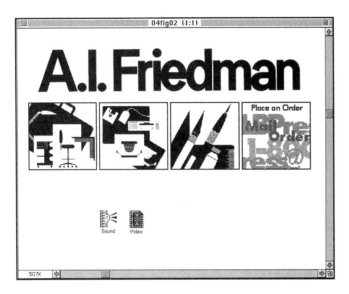

Graphics, sound, or video files are not actually part of the HTML document, however, their titles are used. The file title and location (also called a *path*) tell the browser what to retrieve and where to find it (see page 66).

The browser combines the formatted text with inline graphics and highlights the linked elements. It displays them on your screen as a graphical point-and-click interface.

17

Different Browsers

All browsers perform the same basic functions: they send requests to remote Web servers, receive the data, and display formatted HTML files on your computer screen. But that's where the similarity ends. Some don't do anything else. In fact, they don't even display proportional fonts or graphics. These are called *non-graphical browsers*. Others have features beyond the basics. They display graphics and forms, send e-mail, download files via FTP, and play sound and video. These are called *graphical browsers*.

You must use a browser written for your operating system. Browsers are available for all major systems. You can download a browser at one of the FTP sites listed in the following table (some of these browsers are free; others need to be paid for if you continue to use them).

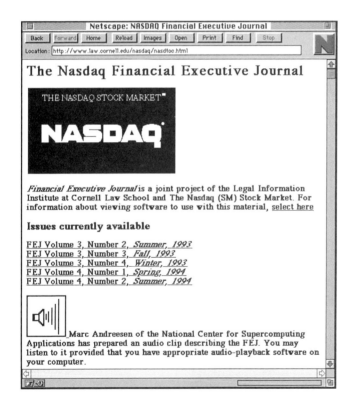

Graphical browsers format text with proportional fonts. They insert inline graphics and highlight hypertext links in color. The browser displays all the text and graphic elements on your screen in a point-and-click interface.

Browser	Platforms Supported	FTP Address	Directory
Netscape	Windows, Macintosh, UNIX	**ftp.netscape.com**	/netscape
Mosaic	Windows, Macintosh, UNIX	**ftp.ncsa.uiuc.edu**	/Web/Mosaic
DOS Lynx	DOS	**ftp2.cc.ukans.edu**	/pub/WWW/DosLynx
Lynx	UNIX	**sunsite.unc.edu**	/pub/packages/info-systems/WWW/clients/lynx
MacWeb	Mac	**ftp.einet.net**	/einet
WinWeb	Windows	**ftp.einet.net**	/einet

Non-graphical browsers usually display text with monospaced fonts. They substitute alternate text for inline graphics.

What's Out There?

A great variety of information, products, and services are available on the Web. Sources range from government to industry, from commerce to colleges, and from publishers to research institutes.

If the source is the United States government, the information—whether text, sound, video, or imagery—is public domain. You can use it any way you want (because our tax dollars paid for it in the first place). This doesn't apply to everything across the board, however, because some information may have been privately funded but made available through government sources by special arrangement. Files should have information to clarify possible uses. Check with the agency making the material available if you are unsure of its public domain status.

Lots of free software and support is available on the Web. Some of it is product specific and supplied by individual hardware manufacturers.

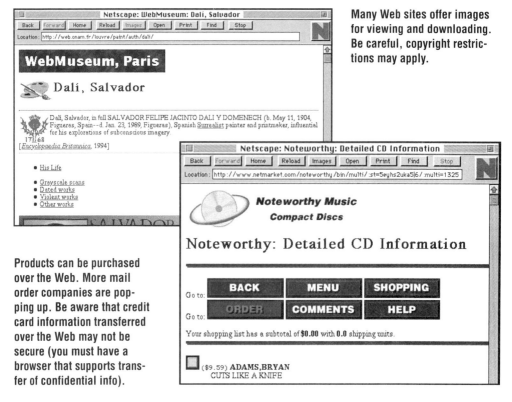

Many Web sites offer images for viewing and downloading. Be careful, copyright restrictions may apply.

Products can be purchased over the Web. More mail order companies are popping up. Be aware that credit card information transferred over the Web may not be secure (you must have a browser that supports transfer of confidential info).

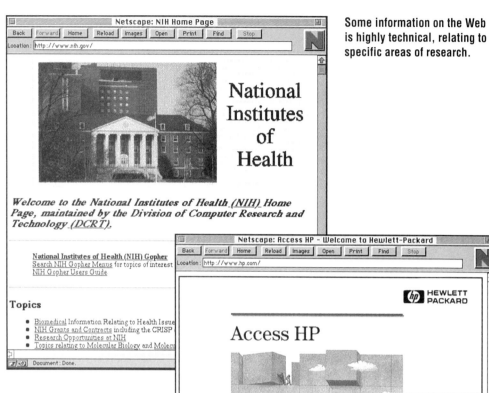

Some information on the Web is highly technical, relating to specific areas of research.

Large corporations are setting up Web sites to promote their products and provide customer service.

Automated indexes help you search databases and locate information.

What You Need to Learn

There are four criteria you need to fulfill to become an HTML electronic publisher: you need to get the right hardware and software; learn the HTML programming language; understand how to structure Web Documents; and find a server to post your pages on. Don't panic. None of these are rocket science.

If you have a computer and you are on the Net already, you probably have this area covered. If you intend to include graphics, sound, and video in your documents, you will need software to create or manipulate these files (see page 24).

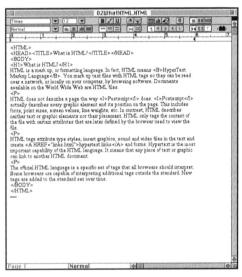

If you know how to type, you can program using HTML. The catch is you just have to know *what* to type (see pages 28-83).

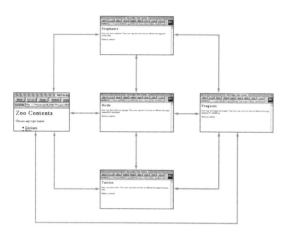

There are only two choices when structuring documents: linear, like a book, and non-linear, like a road map (see pages 84-89). Use linear structures to control the order in which information is viewed, for example, a lesson. Use non-linear structures (as shown here) to allow a person to determine the order in which they view the information from the possibilities you provide, for example, a table of contents.

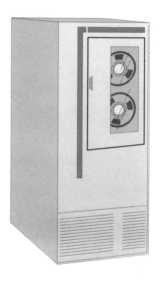

When you find a server to post your pages on, you can download your files and customize any gateway scripts needed. A system administrator can do the parts you don't know how to complete (see page 120).

What You Need to Write or Browse

Writing for the Web and browsing it require some of the same hardware and software, depending on what you want to do. You can write documents that use text and no graphics, sound, or video. You can also browse without the graphics, sound, and video. It's up to you.

To write HTML files, you really only need a word processor, as HTML files are just text files. However, you may want to get HTML authoring software that is

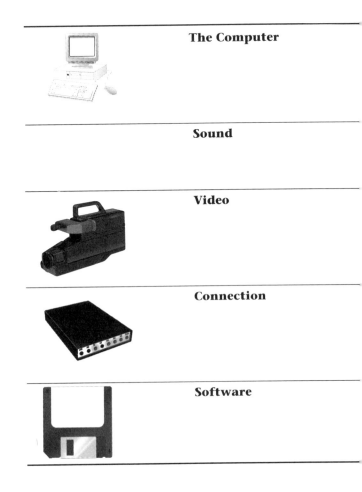

The Computer

Sound

Video

Connection

Software

designed to automate some of the typing (see pages 104-119). To create or edit graphics, sound, and video, you need to have the appropriate hardware and software for working with these files.

To browse, you need a browser program for your operating system, a connection to an access provider, and whatever additional hardware and software that may be needed to view the graphics, sound, and video files you encounter.

Writing	Browsing
Almost any computer that runs a word processor will do.	Processor speed and RAM are the most important factors no matter what platform you choose. Buy or upgrade as much as you can afford.
Sound board and audio software only if you intend to create and edit files.	Sound board and audio software only if you intend to listen to sound when included in files.
Video board and software only if you intend to create and edit files.	Video board and software only if you intend to watch movies when included in files.
No connection is needed to write or post files to a server, you can send them to the server on disk. Often a large project with many graphics would be impractical to move any other way.	You must have a connection to an Internet access provider (the faster the better).
Any word processing software that saves text files will do for HTML programming, or use HTML authoring software. To check your files locally you will need a browser.	Any graphic or non-graphical browser for your platform. Sound and video players if you intend to view these.

Connections

You connect to the Internet via a data transmission line. Lines vary in speed and cost: the faster the line the more expensive the cost. The chart on this page lists options in increasing speed and expense. Localtalk and Ethernet are included in the chart for comparison because they do not connect to the Internet directly, but are used in local area networks. Transmission speed is limited by the slowest link between your computer and the Internet.

Check with the network administrator where you work or study before you spend any money. Most large corporations, government agencies, research institutes, and colleges and universities have high-speed lines connecting their network to the Internet. Ask the network administrator for information about how to use them.

Type	Speed	User
Modem 14.4 Baud, dial-up connection to access provider	14.4 Kilobits/second, about 1.5 pages of text	individual at home or in the office, used for all Internet services
Modem 28.8 Baud, dial-up connection to access provider	28.8 Kilobits/second, about 3 pages of text	individual at home or in the office, used for all Internet services
switch 56, dedicated line, connected to point of presence	56 Kilobits/second, about 6 pages of text	corporations
ISDN, dedicated line, connected to point of presence	64 Kilobits/second, about 8 pages of text	corporations
Localtalk, local area network, must connect to point of presence	230 Kilobits/second, about 25 pages of text	corporations, businesses, schools
T1, dedicated line, connected to point of presence	1.54 Megabits/second, a short book	corporations, research institutes, universities
Ethernet, local area network, must connect to point of presence	10 Megabits/second, a long book	corporations, research institutes, universities
T3, dedicated line, connected to point of presence	45 Megabits/second, the complete works of Shakespeare	corporations, research institutes, universities
FDDI, dedicated line, connected to point of presence	45 Megabits/second, the Oxford English Dictionary	corporations, research institutes, universities

A simple modem plugged into your telephone jack is the least expensive connection method, but it is also the slowest. You can set up the equipment yourself and have the monthly Internet access fees charged to a credit card. If you can only afford a dial-up connection to an Internet access provider, get a fast modem. Spending a little more for the fastest modem will save you money in the long run. A faster modem means quicker data transfers, shorter connect times, and lower bills.

High-end dedicated lines are expensive but fast. Speed allows not only faster transmission time, but also more people to work at the same time. Large corporations and universities can afford a dedicated line like a T1 connection. These involve special equipment and software between your network and the Internet's closest point of presence.

Provider	Cost
purchased by user	local call rates of your telephone company
Purchased by user	local call rates of your telephone company
local telecommunications company	dependent on distance, charged per mile per month
local telecommunications company	dependent on distance, charged per mile per month
corporations, businesses, schools	cost of installation
corporations, research institutes, universities, government	dependent on distance, charged per mile per month
corporations, research institutes, universities, government	cost of installation
corporations, research institutes, universities, government	dependent on distance, charged per mile per month
corporations, research institutes, universities, government	dependent on distance, charged per mile per month

Basic HTML Programming Elements

HTML documents consist of two basic parts: the head and the body. Both the head and the body use pieces of code called tags. *Tags* style text, link files, embed graphics, and create forms, which are used for gathering information from the user.

Some tags can be used by themselves, like **<P>**, the tag that ends a paragraph. Other tags must be used together; for example, to style a first level heading requires opening and closing tags, **<H1>** and **</H1>**. Closing tags contain a slash. Tags for linking files and creating forms require additional parts (also called *arguments*) to work properly. Tags for graphics also require additional parts like the file name and directions for alignment.

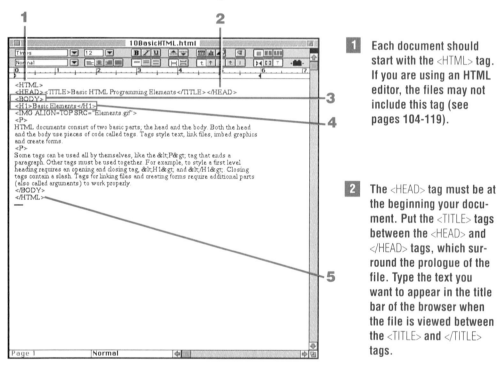

1 Each document should start with the <HTML> tag. If you are using an HTML editor, the files may not include this tag (see pages 104-119).

2 The <HEAD> tag must be at the beginning your document. Put the <TITLE> tags between the <HEAD> and </HEAD> tags, which surround the prologue of the file. Type the text you want to appear in the title bar of the browser when the file is viewed between the <TITLE> and </TITLE> tags.

3 Place the rest of your document between the <BODY> and </BODY> tags.

4 The <H1> and </H1> tags surround the text that appears in the first level heading style.

5 End every document with </HTML>.

28

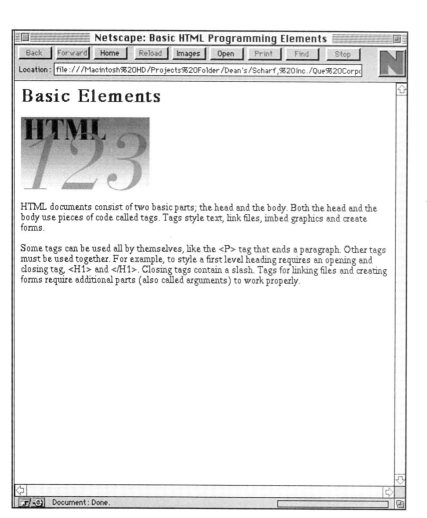

Basic Elements

HTML documents consist of two basic parts; the head and the body. Both the head and the body use pieces of code called tags. Tags style text, link files, imbed graphics and create forms.

Some tags can be used all by themselves, like the <P> tag that ends a paragraph. Other tags must be used together. For example, to style a first level heading requires an opening and closing tag, <H1> and </H1>. Closing tags contain a slash. Tags for linking files and creating forms require additional parts (also called arguments) to work properly.

Relative Type Styles

One way to style type is with *relative tags*. These include six heading tags (H1 through H6) and tags like strong and emphasis. Each tag indicates a style set in the browser preferences. Styles vary from browser to browser, but generally have the same characteristics (see page 18).

Heading styles H1 through H6 start large and bold and gradually lessen in size and weight. H5 and H6 style preferences can be very different from those in the browser you use. You may get a result you don't like, so it is a good idea to stay away from them.

H1 is the largest and boldest; use it for the most important type on your page. H2 is smaller and less bold; use it for sub-heads. H3 is smaller and carries less weight than H1 or H2; use it when you need to have a third level of heading. Use H4, H5, and H6 sparingly. You do not want your page to look like an outline (unless, of course, it is).

Address is often italic and is meant for e-mail, phone numbers, and postal addresses. The tag for address is **<ADDRESS>**.

Emphasis and *strong* draw the eye to the type, usually by making it bold or italic. These are marked with the **<EM>** and **<STRONG>** tags.

Code, sample, and *keyboard* format type in a monospaced font, usually Courier. These are marked with the **<CODE>**, **<SAMP>**, and **<KBD>** tags.

If you do not indicate a type style, the text will be formatted in plain type. All of these type-style tags are used in pairs. The closing tags for heading styles insert a paragraph break automatically. Other text styles, often used within copy, do not.

1 Start with an opening tag in front of the text.

2 Put the text you want to style between the tags.

3 End with a closing tag after the text.

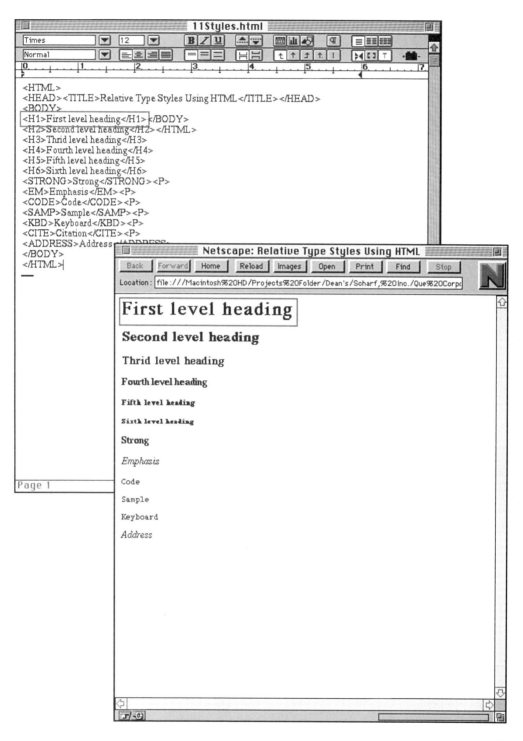

Fixed Type Styles

One way to style type is with *fixed tags*. Unlike relative style tags for heading levels or emphasis, each of these tags indicates a type style that does not vary from browser to browser.

If you do not indicate any type style, the text will be formatted in plain type.

The various fixed type styles and their tags are:

Style	Tag
Bold	**\<B\>**
Italic	**\<I\>**
Underscore	**\<U\>**
Typewriter	**\<TT\>**

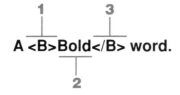

1. Start with an opening tag in front of the text.

2. Put the text you want to style between the tags.

3. End with a closing tag after the text.

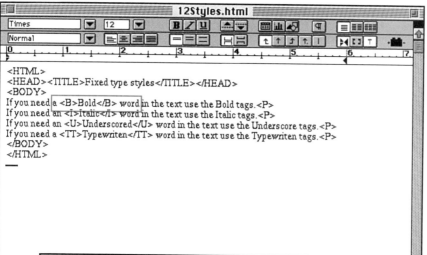

```
<HTML>
<HEAD><TITLE>Fixed type styles</TITLE></HEAD>
<BODY>
If you need a <B>Bold</B> word in the text use the Bold tags.<P>
If you need an <I>Italic</I> word in the text use the Italic tags.<P>
If you need an <U>Underscored</U> word in the text use the Underscore tags.<P>
If you need a <TT>Typewriten</TT> word in the text use the Typewriten tags.<P>
</BODY>
</HTML>
```

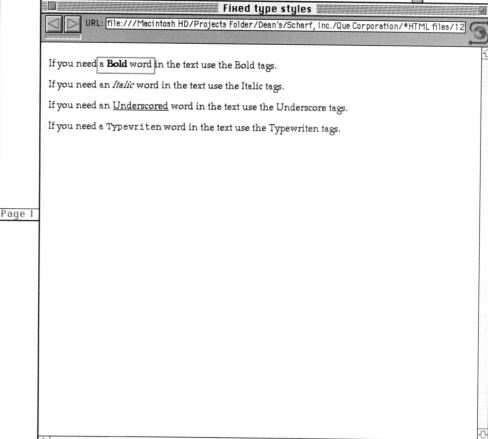

If you need a **Bold** word in the text use the Bold tags.

If you need an *Italic* word in the text use the Italic tags.

If you need an <u>Underscored</u> word in the text use the Underscore tags.

If you need a Typewriten word in the text use the Typewriten tags.

Line and Paragraph Breaks

The line break tag, **
, ends a line whether following text or graphics. The paragraph break tag, **<P>, ends a line and inserts a line space that separates elements visually. Both tags are used alone, not in pairs like the **<B>** and **</B>** tags.

You must insert a tag when you want to break a line or end a paragraph in a specific place. Otherwise, the text will flow to fit the width of the browser window, and will break differently when the browser window is resized.

There are plenty of other good reasons to break lines and paragraphs. Breaking large copy blocks into smaller concise segments helps readability. Obviously, you will want to break lines of poetry and address blocks.

**There are plenty of other good reasons to break
**

**lines
** —————2

**and
**

paragraphs.

<P> —————1

Breaking large copy into smaller blocks.

1 <P> **ends a paragraph and adds a line space.**

2
 ends a line without adding any space.

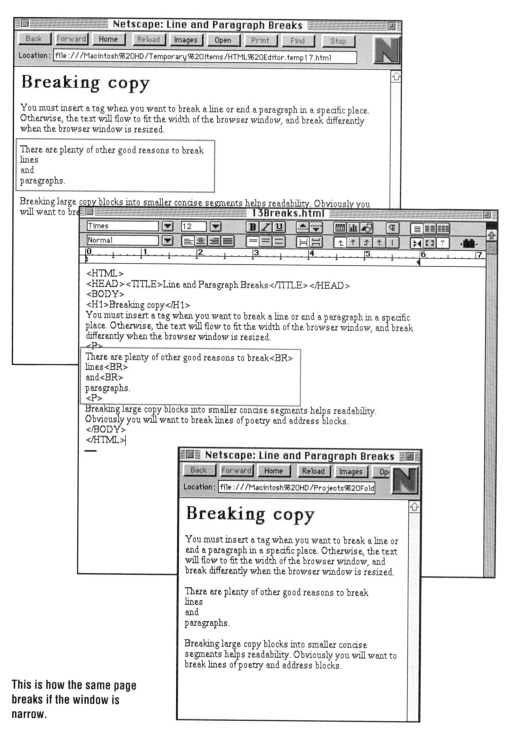

This is how the same page breaks if the window is narrow.

Text Links

Linked text allows a person to click on a word or phrase and jump to another file. This capability is called *hypertext.* The linked text shows up in color and is underscored depending on the preference settings of the browser.

Type the example below exactly the way it appears to create a link to a file named Art.html. To make your own linked text, just substitute the file name and the copy that gets clicked to whatever you want. Page 46 shows when to use just a file name and when to use a full path.

1. Start with the opening tag <A HREF= in front of the file name. Think of the <A as meaning anchor and HREF as meaning hypertext reference.

2. Put the file name you want to link between the quote marks.

3. Put the text you want people to click on the screen between the > and < symbols.

4. End with a closing tag </A> after the text.

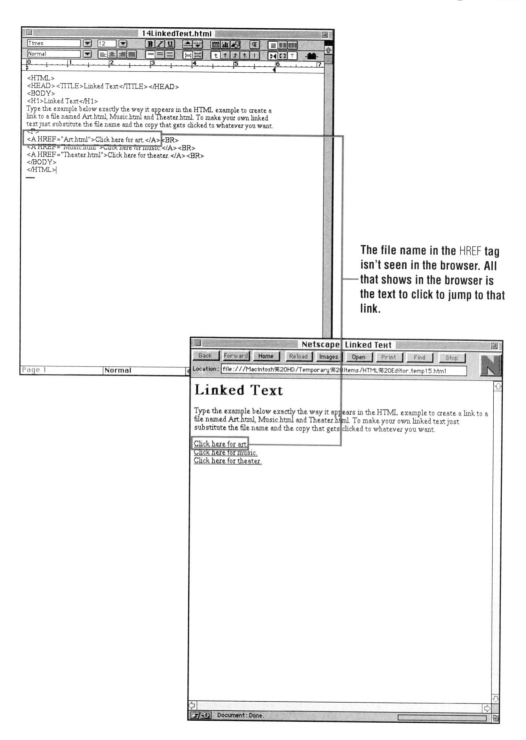

The file name in the HREF tag isn't seen in the browser. All that shows in the browser is the text to click to jump to that link.

Graphic Links

Linked graphics allow a person to click on an image and jump to another file. This capability can make your documents easier to use. Good clear graphics communicate quickly and enhance the usability of your document. The linked graphic shows up outlined in color depending on the preference settings of the browser.

To link a graphic, type the same code as for linked text. In place of the clickable text, insert a graphic for users to click.

Type the example below exactly the way it appears to create a link to a file named Art.html. To make your own linked graphic, just substitute the file name and the image that gets clicked with your own file name and image.

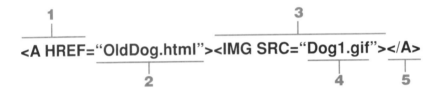

1 Start with the opening tag `<A HREF=` in front of the file name.

2 Put the file name you want to link between the quote marks.

3 Put the `<IMG>` tag (the tag that inserts a graphic on the screen, see page 52) between the > and < symbols of the link tag. Think of IMG as meaning image.

4 Put the file name of the image you want people to click between the quote marks of the `<IMG>` tag.

5 End with a closing tag `</A>` for the link after the last part of the `<IMG>` tag.

38

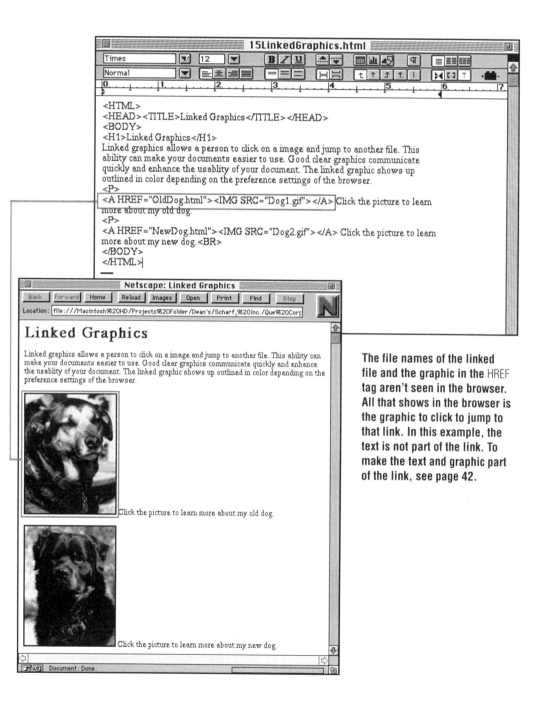

The file names of the linked file and the graphic in the HREF tag aren't seen in the browser. All that shows in the browser is the graphic to click to jump to that link. In this example, the text is not part of the link. To make the text and graphic part of the link, see page 42.

FTP and E-Mail

Browsers can retrieve files by using anonymous FTP to connect to the FTP servers. Just put the complete URL of the file you want to get as the file name of the link. When someone clicks the link for the file in their browser, the browser connects to the FTP server and saves the file to their hard disk.

Some browsers also send e-mail. Put the complete e-mail address as the file name of a link. When a person clicks on the link, a dialog box will appear for the subject and body of the message.

The format for the address that you link to uses URLs. The URL includes the type of service, the address, the path, and the file name. You can use this same technique shown here for FTP servers to connect to Gopher and UseNet news. The URL codes for the most popular Internet services are on top of the following page.

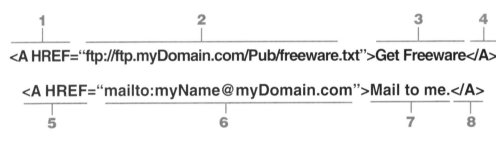

1 Start with the opening tag in front of the URL. **2** Put the complete URL of the file you want to retrieve between the quote marks. This includes the URL code for FTP (ftp://), the address of the FTP server (ftp.myDomain.com), the path (/Pub/), and the file name (freeware.txt). FTP paths and file names can be case sensitive, so use the correct capitalization.	**3** Put the text you want people to click on between the > and < symbols. **4** End with a closing tag after the text. **5** Start with the opening tag in front of the mail address. **6** Put the complete URL of the person you want to send a message to between the quote marks. The URL is mailto: followed by their e-mail address.	**7** Put the text you want people to click on between the > and < symbols. **8** End with a closing tag after the text.

Internet Service	URL Code
World Wide Web	http://
FTP	ftp://
Gopher	gopher://
Mail	mailto: (Not all browsers support this.)
UseNet News	news:

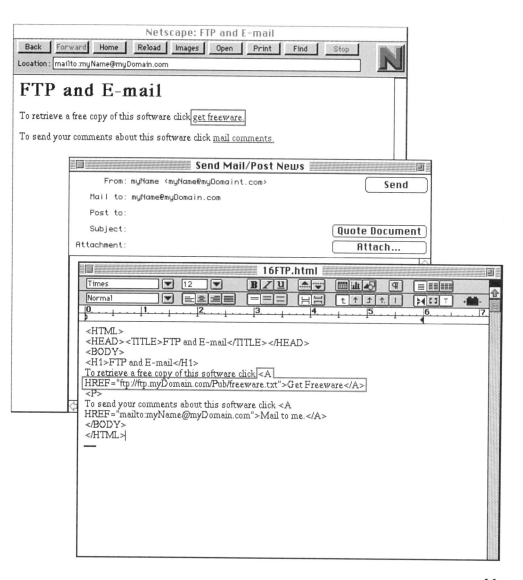

Alternatives to Images for Non-Graphical Browsers

People using non-graphical browsers, like Lynx, and people who turn off the image loading in graphical browsers do not see in-line graphics on their screens. They only see text in Lynx, the word [IMAGE] replaces the graphic. If you want them to know what graphic you inserted, you have a problem.

The solution is an extended version of the **<IMG>** tag. The **<ALT>** tag allows you to include a description of the graphic. This descriptive copy substitutes for the graphic. It is a good idea to do this for all graphics.

Another alternative here is to simply include a separate text link following the graphic link for any picture. That way, people using browsers that don't support the **<ALT>** tag will still have a link to use.

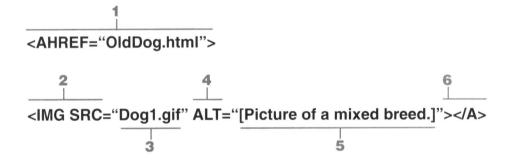

1 Start with <AHREF="OldDog.html"> to create a link. The text between the quotes is the file name you link to (see page 38).

2 Put the <IMG SRC= tag in front of the graphic file-name. Think of IMG as meaning image and SRC as meaning source.

3 Put the graphic file name between the quote marks.

4 Put the <ALT> tag after the name of the graphic file. Think of ALT as meaning alternate.

5 Put the descriptive copy that substitutes for the graphic between the quotes of the <ALT> tag.

6 End with the > symbol to close the <IMG> tag and </A> to close the link tag. The <IMG> tag does not end with </IMG>. It is not paired like the <B> and </B> tags. SRC and ALT are arguments to the IMG tag and lie within the <IMG> and the closing > symbol.

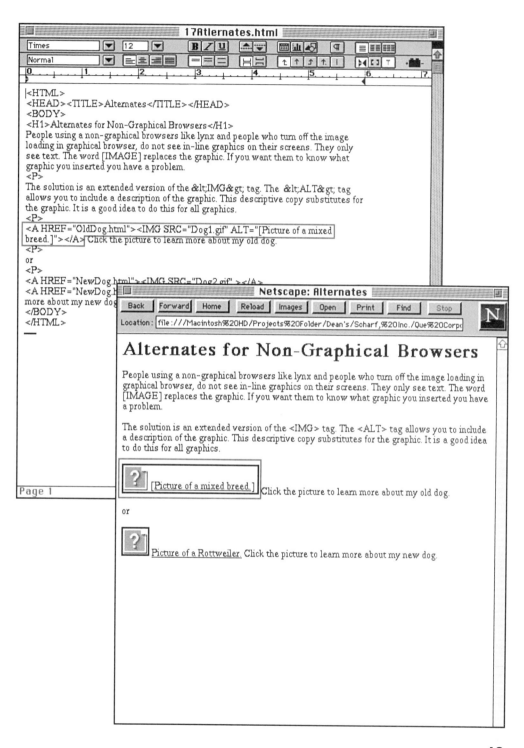

Links within Documents

Text and graphics can link to places within the same document. These links require two parts: the anchor and the link. The *anchor* identifies the place to jump to. The *link* uses the name of the anchor instead of the name of a file. (The list items used in the example code here are explained on pages 58-61.)

Link

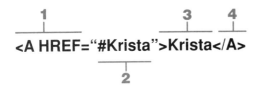

1 Start with the opening tag <A HREF= in front of the anchor name.

2 Put a # symbol followed by the anchor name you want to link to between the quote marks.

3 Put the text you want people to click on between the > and < symbols.

4 End with a closing tag </A> after the text.

Anchor

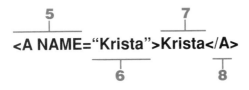

5 Start with the opening tag <A NAME= in front of the anchor name.

6 Put the name of the anchor between the quote marks.

7 Put the text that appears on the screen between the > and < symbols.

8 End with a closing tag </A> behind the text.

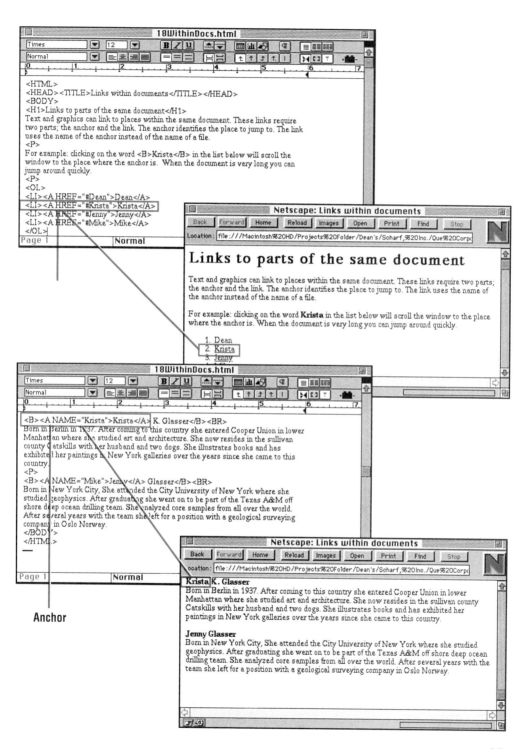

Anchor

Relative and Absolute Path Names

A URL describes the location of a file. A complete URL includes the name of the server, disk, and all the directories within which a file resides. URLs are also called *paths*. There are two types of paths.

Absolute paths spell out the location of a file by starting at the highest level and listing each directory needed to find the file. You start the path with the type of service, which is http:// for Web pages, followed by the name of the server, a slash (/), and the exact name of each directory and the file (i.e. http://myDomain.com/abcFolder/xyzFile.html). Separate each directory with a slash. Getting one part of the URL wrong means the file won't be found. You will have to change paths in your document if a disk or directory name changes.

Relative paths spell out the location of a file based on the current document location. When you use a file name like xyzfile.html, you are using a relative URL. In this case, the browser looks for the file in the same directory as the current document. If it is not there, the file won't be found. When you type **../** in front of the file name (i.e., ../xyzfile.html), the browser looks for the file in the directory one level above the current document. When you type **../../** in front of the file name (i.e., ../../xyzfile.html), the browser looks for the file in the directory two levels above the current document.

Web URLs are case sensitive, so be sure to use proper capitalization.

1 The file name.

2 The directory names are separated by slashes.

3 Using ../ indicates a directory level above the current directory.

URL	Where the Referenced File Is Found
xyzFile.html	The HTML file named xyzfile.html is found in the current directory
abcFolder/xyzFile.html	The HTML file named xyzfile.html is found in the directory named abcFolder in the current directory
http://myDomain.com /abcFolder/xyzFile.html	The HTML file named xyzfile.html is found in the directory named abcFolder on the server named myDomain.com
../abcFolder/xyzFile.html	The HTML file named xyzfile.html is found in the directory named abcFolder one directory level above the current directory
../../abcFolder/xyzFile.html	The HTML file named xyzfile.html is found in the directory named abcFolder two directory levels above the current directory

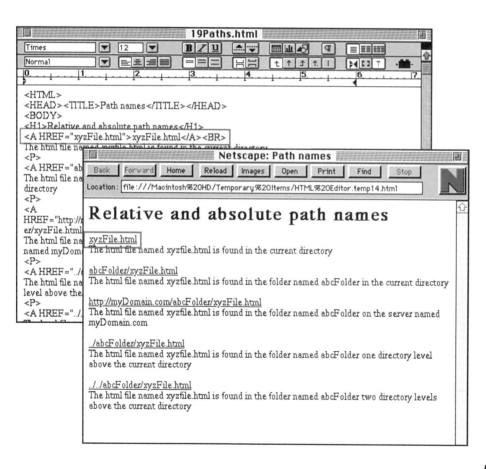

Block Quotes

One way to style type so that it stands out from the rest of your copy is by using the **<BLOCKQUOTE>** tag. This tag will indent the text. You will still have to use the **<P>** and **
** tags to break paragraphs and lines in particular places (see page 34).

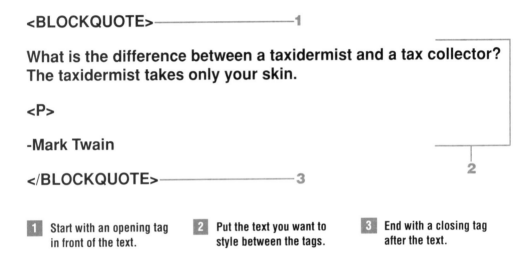

<BLOCKQUOTE>————————1

What is the difference between a taxidermist and a tax collector? The taxidermist takes only your skin.

<P>

-Mark Twain

</BLOCKQUOTE>————————3

2

1 Start with an opening tag in front of the text.

2 Put the text you want to style between the tags.

3 End with a closing tag after the text.

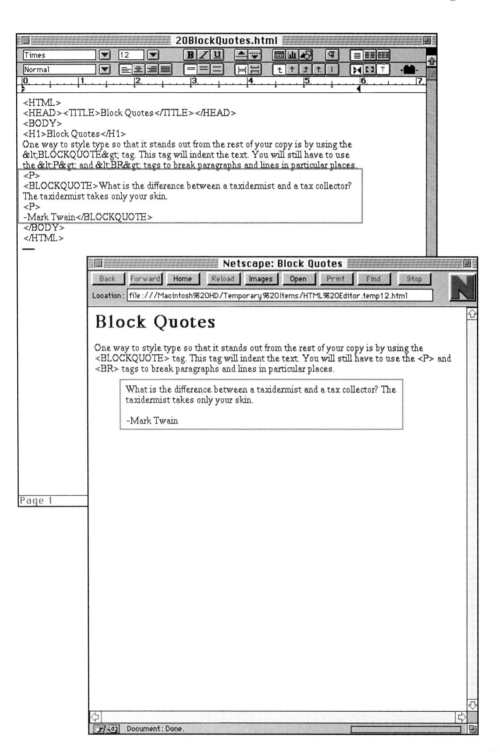

Dividing Rules

One way to divide documents into sections is by using rules. The **<HR>** tag inserts a rule that stretches completely across the screen. The rule will break the copy wherever it is inserted. It will appear black and scale to the same width as the browser window. Think of the **<HR>** as meaning "horizontal rule."

Another way to divide documents into sections is by using graphics as rules. You make the graphic rule in a paint program and insert it with the **<IMG>** tag (see page 52). Graphic rules do not change width when the browser screen is resized. The graphic rule will not break the copy unless you use the **<P>** or **
** tags.

Inserting a dividing rule

<HR>————————**1**

Rules are one way to divide documents into sections.

1 The <HR> tag inserts a rule.

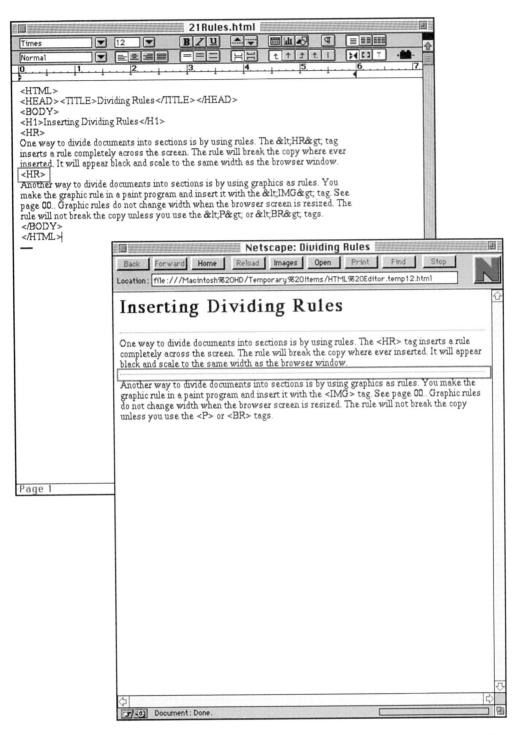

```
<HTML>
<HEAD><TITLE>Dividing Rules</TITLE></HEAD>
<BODY>
<H1>Inserting Dividing Rules</H1>
<HR>
One way to divide documents into sections is by using rules. The &lt;HR&gt; tag
inserts a rule completely across the screen. The rule will break the copy where ever
inserted. It will appear black and scale to the same width as the browser window.
<HR>
Another way to divide documents into sections is by using graphics as rules. You
make the graphic rule in a paint program and insert it with the &lt;IMG&gt; tag. See
page 00.. Graphic rules do not change width when the browser screen is resized. The
rule will not break the copy unless you use the &lt;P&gt; or &lt;BR&gt; tags.
</BODY>
</HTML>
```

Page 1

Netscape: Dividing Rules

Location: file:///Macintosh%20HD/Temporary%20Items/HTML%20Editor.temp12.html

Inserting Dividing Rules

One way to divide documents into sections is by using rules. The <HR> tag inserts a rule completely across the screen. The rule will break the copy where ever inserted. It will appear black and scale to the same width as the browser window.

Another way to divide documents into sections is by using graphics as rules. You make the graphic rule in a paint program and insert it with the <IMG> tag. See page 00.. Graphic rules do not change width when the browser screen is resized. The rule will not break the copy unless you use the <P> or <BR> tags.

Document: Done.

Graphics

Browsers can display graphic images along with text, which makes documents look better. More importantly, images communicate information that would be impossible or too difficult to communicate in words.

You insert a graphic using the **<IMG>** tag and the name of the graphic file. All browsers do not read all file formats. Use the GIF format for saving graphic files; it is read by most graphical browsers.

Remember that graphic files are big. Big graphics mean even bigger files. Documents with large images or many small ones take a long time to transfer over the Web, usually longer than anyone wants to wait. Often the image is not worth the long load time anyway. Use graphics only when they add information or utilities.

Type the example below exactly the way it appears to insert a graphic named Clips1.gif. To insert your own graphic, just substitute the file name with your own. This works for image files in the same directory as the current Web document. You must specify a more specific URL for a graphic if it is not in the same directory (see page 46).

You should decide on a consistent place to keep graphic files, whether that is in the same directory as the HTML files or not, and a consistent method for referring to graphic files. It is good practice to indicate where the files are with a more specific URL. This guarantees that the graphic files will always be found.

1 Start with the opening tag <IMG SRC= in front of the file name. Think of SRC as meaning source.

2 Put the graphic file name you want displayed between the quote marks.

3 End with a closing tag > after the file name.

Rate	Approximate Transfer Time for 100 KB File	
2400	8-10 minutes	10-12 KB per minute
9600	2-4 minutes	40-50 KB per minute
14400	1.5 minutes	60-80 KB per minute

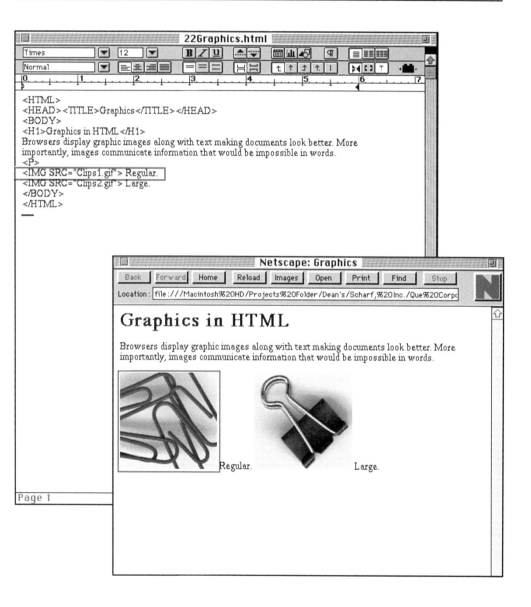

Aligning Graphics

You align graphics with text using the **ALIGN** attribute within the **<IMG>** tag. There are three alignment options: top, middle, and bottom. If you do not specify an alignment, the bottom of the image aligns with the text.

The **ALIGN** attribute controls the graphic, not the text. Try this attribute with a small graphic, like a bullet, in front of large text, like a heading, to see clearly how it works.

The attributes of the **IMG** tag do not have to be in any specific order. For example, <IMG ALIGN=top SRC="dollar.gif" ALT="One"> and <IMG ALT="One" SRC="dollar.gif" ALIGN=top> do the same thing.

Type the example below exactly the way it appears to insert a graphic named dollar.gif. To insert your own graphic, just substitute the file name with your own.

<IMG ALIGN=top SRC="dollar.gif">Align to top of graphic.

1 Start with the opening <IMG **tag.**

2 Put the ALIGN= **attribute next. Choose top, middle, or bottom alignment options, followed by** SRC=.

3 Put the graphic file name you want displayed between the quote marks as the source.

4 End the image tag with a closing > symbol behind the file name.

5 The text can come before or after the image that aligns to it.

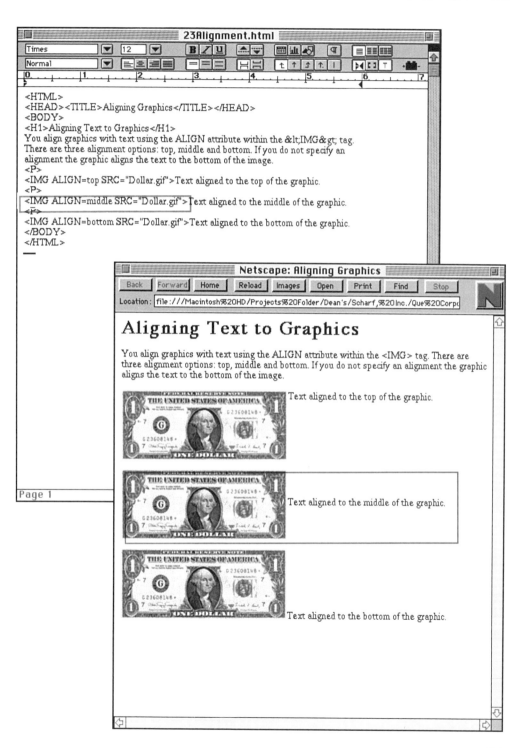

Transparent Graphics

Most GIF file formats are opaque; even the white parts of the image are not transparent. Opaque and transparent images are always rectangular—you cannot change that. However, silhouetted transparent images seem irregularly shaped and float on the background.

You make opaque GIF files transparent by using converter software. Converters for most platforms are available at FTP archives. (The site at **ftp.NCSA.uiuc.edu** has all the converters listed below.) They all work pretty much the same way. Popular image editors that support transparent GIFs for Windows, Mac, and UNIX are:

Platform	Program	Directory and Name at ftp.NCSA.uiuc.edu
Windows	Lview	/Web/Mosaic/Windows/viewers/lviewp1a.zip
Mac	GIF Converter	/Web/Mosaic/Mac/Helpers/gif-converter-237.hqx
UNIX	xv	/Web/Mosaic/Unix/viewers/xv-3.00.tar.Z

Not all images should be transparent. Images with one solid color in the background convert well. Pick appropriate images to avoid odd transparency effects.

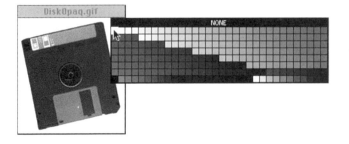

Open the file you want to convert. Choose a color you want to make transparent. Save the file.

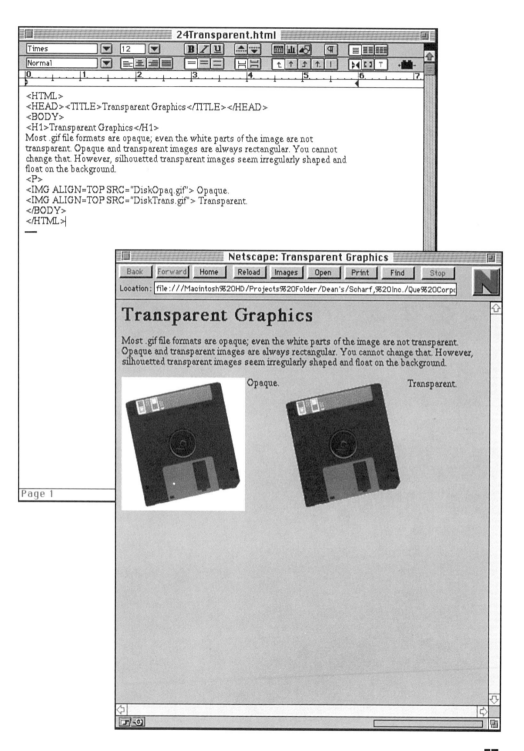

Lists

Lists come in two basic varieties: *ordered* (with numbers), and *unordered* (with bullets). Both kinds indent the list from the rest of the copy. You can nest lists within each other, as in an outline. The nested list indents from the list it sits in.

Identify ordered lists with the **<OL>** tag and unordered lists with the **<UL>** tag. Both lists use the **<LI>** tag for items in the list. The **<OL>** and **<UL>** tags are paired. The **<LI>** tag is used by itself.

Sometimes you see Web documents with small graphics in lists instead of numbers or bullets. The person who wrote the document inserted small graphics with the **<IMG>** tag (see page 52).

This is an ordered list. It has numbers in front of every list item.

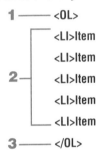

1 ——— <OL>

        <LI>Item

        <LI>Item

2   <LI>Item

        <LI>Item

        <LI>Item

3 ——— </OL>

This is an unordered list. It has bullets in front of every list item.

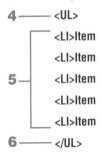

4 ——— <UL>

        <LI>Item

        <LI>Item

5   <LI>Item

        <LI>Item

        <LI>Item

6 ——— </UL>

1 Start by inserting the <OL> tag in front of the first item in the list.

2 Put the <LI> tag in front of every item in the list. Numbers appear automatically, so you don't need to type them in.

3 Put the </OL> tag after the last item in the list.

4 Start by inserting the <UL> tag in front of the first item in the list.

5 Put the <LI> tag in front of every item in the list. Bullets appear automatically, so you don't need to type them in.

6 Finish by inserting the </UL> tag after the last item in the list.

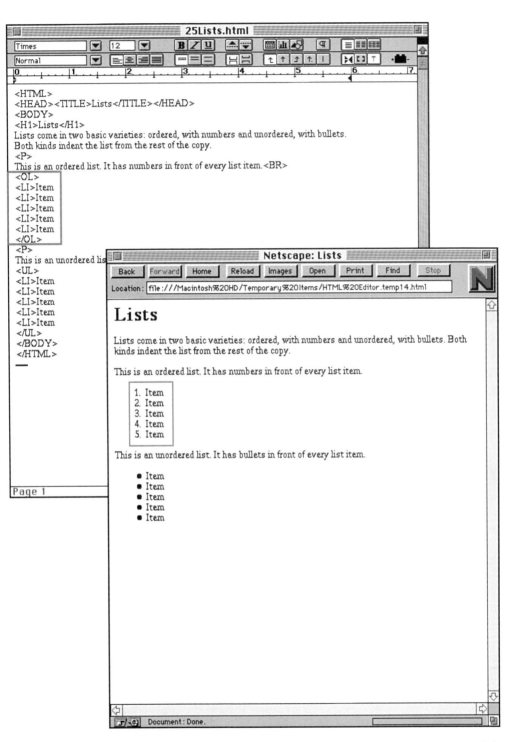

Definition Lists

Definition lists are meant for lists that have two parts, such as a term in a glossary, but they can be used for any similar situation. Definition lists don't have numbers or bullets, so you need to type them as part of the copy. The **<DL>** tag is used to identify the list, **<DT>** is used for each term, and **<DD>** is used for the definition part. The **<DL>** tag is paired, the **<DT>** and **<DD>** tags are not. To help you remember the tags, think of **<DL>** as meaning definition list, **<DT>** as definition term, and **<DD>** as definition description.

<DL>————————**1**
<DT>Term————————**2**
<DD>The definition of the term. If the definition is a long one the copy will wrap to fit in the window width. The copy continues to indent as part of the definition. Each term starts on a new line. ⎤**3**
<DT>Term
<DD>The definition of the term. If the definition is a long one the copy will wrap to fit in the window width. The copy continues to indent as part of the definition. Each term starts on a new line.
</DL>————————**4**

1 Start by placing the <DL> tag in front of the first item in the definition list.

2 Put the <DT> tag in front of every term in the list.

3 Put the <DD> tag in front of every definition in the list.

4 End by putting the </DL> tag after the last item in the definition list.

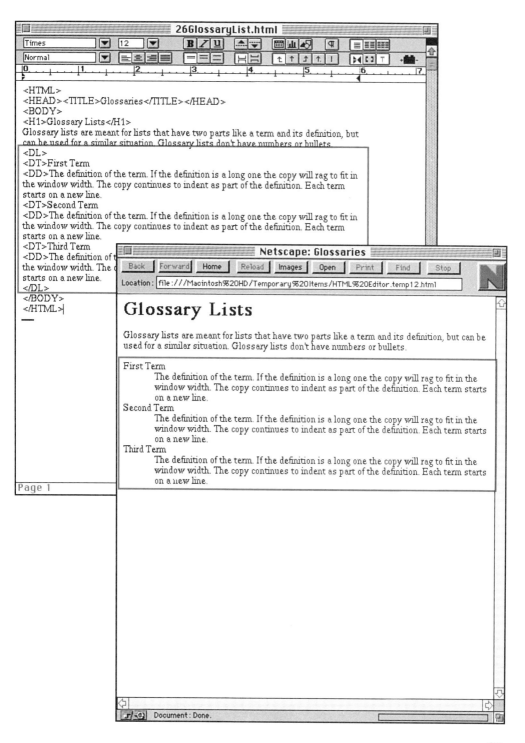

Special and Reserved Characters

The only characters you can type in HTML documents are the letters, numbers, and symbols that appear on your keyboard. Any character that you type by holding down a key other than the Shift key may not work when someone views your document over the Web. That's because not every computer uses the same combination of keys to mean the same special character. Bullets, accented letters, ©, ™, ®, å, π, £, and ¢ fall into the special character set.

The HTML language reserves some characters for code only, for example, the ", &, <, and > symbols. You cannot type a reserved character directly in the text of your document.

Use named or numbered entities whenever you need a special or reserved character in the text of your document. Named entities use abbreviations, while numbered entities use the ASCII numbers to indicate the character (see page 144) for an ASCII list).

Named Entities

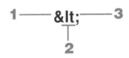

1 Start with an & in front of the abbreviation.

2 Put the abbreviation next.

3 End with a ; (semicolon) after the abbreviation.

Numbered Entities

4 Start with an &# in front of the ASCII number.

5 Put the ASCII number next.

6 End with a ; after the ASCII number.

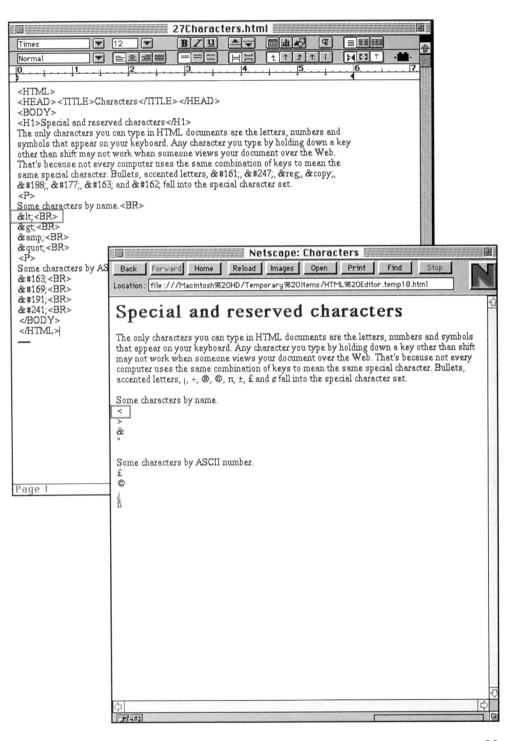

Preformatted Type

A browser normally formats the text in an HTML file and ignores any extra spaces, tabs, or line returns you add to the file. The **<PRE>** tag, however, formats the text based on the way you type it. It retains all the spaces, tabs, and returns in the HTML file so that it looks exactly the same when viewed with a browser. There's one catch: The text appears in monospaced type, like Courier. Charts are usually created with the **<PRE>** tag. Always use a monospaced font when creating preformatted text so that the spacing reflects the final display in the browser.

<PRE> ————————————————————————————————— 1

Units sold

	April	May	June	July	August
Pencils	300	1000	300	200	100
Pads	400	2000	400	300	200
Erasers	500	3000	500	400	300
Paper clips	600	4000	600	500	400

</PRE> ———————————————————————————————— 3

1 Start by putting the <PRE> tag in front of the text.

2 Put the text you want to style between the tags.

3 Put the </PRE> tag after the text.

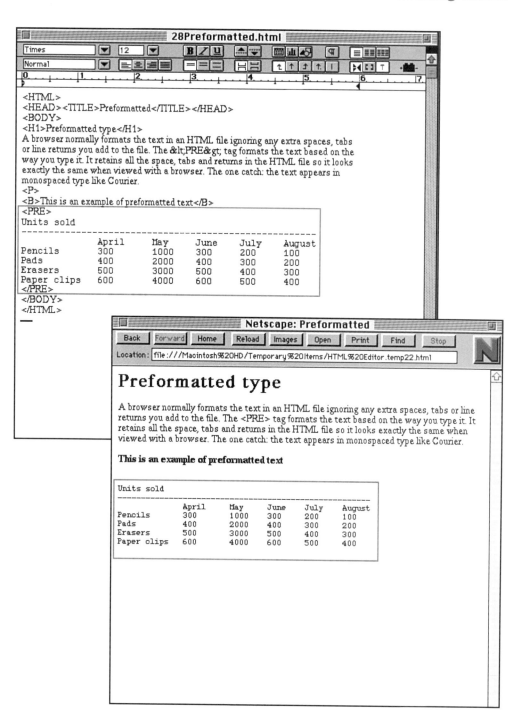

28Preformatted.html

```
<HTML>
<HEAD><TITLE>Preformatted</TITLE></HEAD>
<BODY>
<H1>Preformatted type</H1>
A browser normally formats the text in an HTML file ignoring any extra spaces, tabs
or line returns you add to the file. The &lt;PRE&gt; tag formats the text based on the
way you type it. It retains all the space, tabs and returns in the HTML file so it looks
exactly the same when viewed with a browser. The one catch: the text appears in
monospaced type like Courier.
<P>
<B>This is an example of preformatted text</B>
<PRE>
Units sold
-----------------------------------------------------------------
            April     May       June      July      August
Pencils     300       1000      300       200       100
Pads        400       2000      400       300       200
Erasers     500       3000      500       400       300
Paper clips 600       4000      600       500       400
</PRE>
</BODY>
</HTML>
```

Netscape: Preformatted

Back | Forward | Home | Reload | Images | Open | Print | Find | Stop

Location: file:///Macintosh%20HD/Temporary%20Items/HTML%20Editor.temp22.html

Preformatted type

A browser normally formats the text in an HTML file ignoring any extra spaces, tabs or line returns you add to the file. The <PRE> tag formats the text based on the way you type it. It retains all the space, tabs and returns in the HTML file so it looks exactly the same when viewed with a browser. The one catch: the text appears in monospaced type like Courier.

This is an example of preformatted text

```
Units sold
-----------------------------------------------------------------
            April     May       June      July      August
Pencils     300       1000      300       200       100
Pads        400       2000      400       300       200
Erasers     500       3000      500       400       300
Paper clips 600       4000      600       500       400
```

Sound and Video

It is possible to include sound and video in your HTML documents. You insert sound and video files as you do linked text or graphics.

Browsers do not play sound or video, they only retrieve the file. Another program takes over from there, and that's one of the problems. You don't know if the people trying to see or hear your file have the right software and hardware. If they do, it is still hard to choose a file format available for all platforms. The best you can do is tell them the file format you picked and let them determine whether or not they can use it.

There are very few cross-platform file formats. For sound, AIFF for the Macintosh and WAV for Windows are common formats. For video, the MPEG format is common and viewers are available for Windows, Mac, and UNIX. QuickTime is also a common format that can be viewed in Windows and Macs. You may opt for other formats, just remember to mention whichever you choose in the text.

Remember sound and video files are big. Long clips and higher quality mean even bigger files. Big files take a long time to transfer over the Web. That's why it's a good idea to put the file size in the text so people know how long the file takes to load.

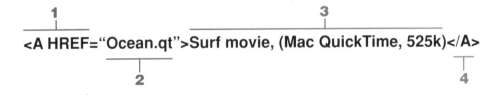

1 Start with the opening tag <A HREF= in front of the file name.

2 Put the file name of the sound or video between the quote marks.

3 Put the text you want people to click on between the > and < symbols. Include the file size and format.

4 End with a closing tag </A> after the text.

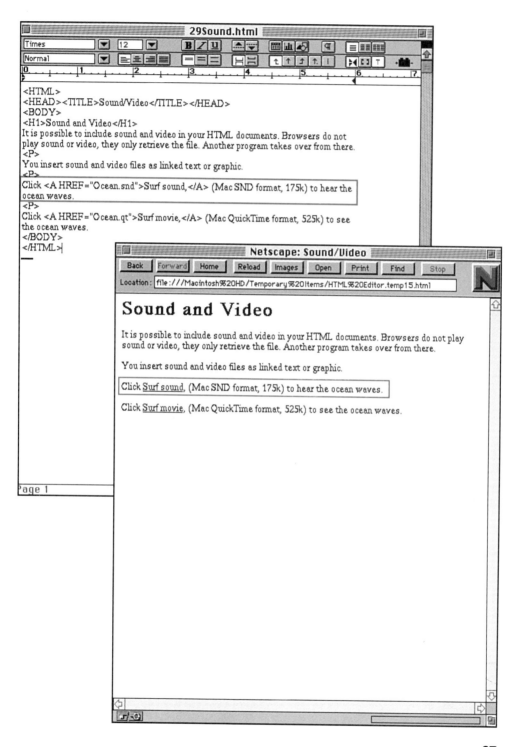

Image Maps

Normally, clicking on any spot on a linked graphic is the same as clicking on another. One link per graphic is the rule. But with *image maps*, a graphic contains more than one link. Clicking on different parts takes you to different files. To function properly, image maps require several files and a gateway script run on the server.

Not every graphic is appropriate for mapping. Choose graphics that have clearly defined sections or labels. Prompts in the text will help people understand that the image on their screen contains multiple links.

Next, create a file containing the coordinates of the different sections of the graphic. If the shape is circular, specify the center of the circle and the radius. If the shape is rectangular, specify the upper-left and lower-right corners of the rectangle. If the shape is a polygon, specify all corner points. If the shape is a single point, specify the point. The upper-left corner of a graphic is 0,0. The format of the coordinates is different depending on the type of server used. If shapes overlap, their order in the coordinate file determines which lies on top.

Last, you need a gateway script available on the server that takes the mouse click coordinates from the browser, looks them up in the coordinate file, and opens the correct link. (Gateway scripts are a complicated matter. If your Web server isn't already set up for this, you may want to check out the Que books *Running a Perfect Web Site* or *Special Edition Using HTML* for further information.)

The link

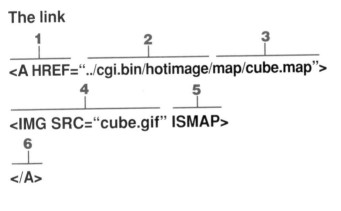

1 Start by creating a link.

2 Put the URL of the gateway script you need here.

3 Put the complete URL of the file containing the map coordinates here.

4 Insert a graphic.

5 Include the argument ISMAP so that the browser knows to send the mouse click coordinates to the gateway script.

6 End with the link's closing tag.

The Coordinate File Following the CERN Standards

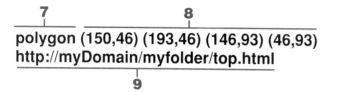

```
polygon (150,46) (193,46) (146,93) (46,93)
http://myDomain/myfolder/top.html
```

7 Start with the type of shape.

8 Put each coordinate needed to describe the shape between parentheses.

9 End with the complete URL of the linked file.

The Coordinate File Following the NCSA Standards

10   **11**

```
polygon http://myDomain/myfolder/top.html
150,46 193,46 146,93 46,93
```
            12

10 Start with the type of shape.

11 Put the complete URL of the linked file next.

12 End with each coordinate needed to describe the shape. Do not use parentheses.

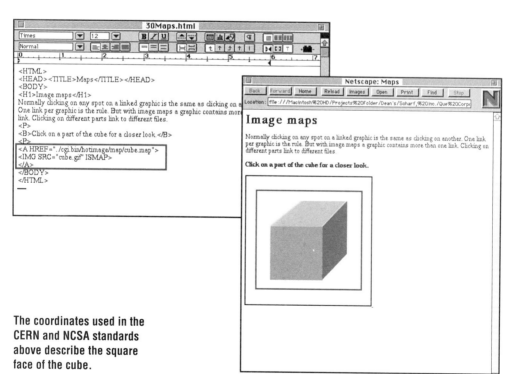

The coordinates used in the CERN and NCSA standards above describe the square face of the cube.

What Is a Form?

A *form* is a special part of the body of an HTML document. It allows users to input text and make choices from check boxes, radio buttons, and selection lists. You design forms for your specific purposes by combining these input types.

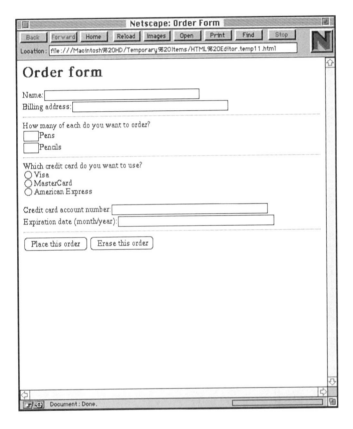

Forms are often literally just that, forms for gathering information. Purchase orders, registration cards, applications, and exams all fall into this category. The browser sends the user input to an e-mail address.

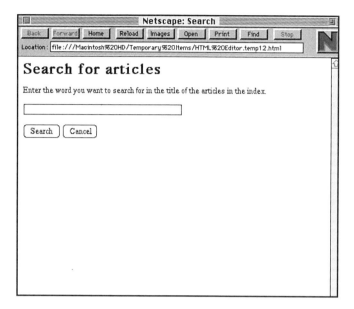

Forms are used for defining search parameters. The browser sends the input to the server for processing. The result returns for display on your screen.

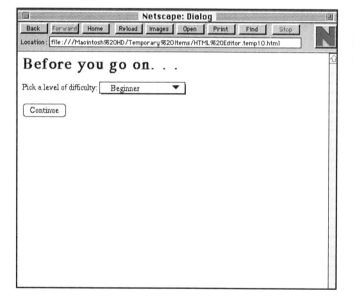

Forms are used for dialog boxes. A choice defines which branch of a document you enter.

How Forms Work

A form works in conjunction with a gateway script on a server to process the information submitted to it. Writing scripts requires a higher level of programming expertise than what is covered in this book. A good source for getting started with gateway scripts is Que's *Special Edition Using HTML* by Tom Savola.

If you don't know any programming languages except HTML, you will find it easier to ask for help from the staff at your server. Ask the staff if they have a script you can use.

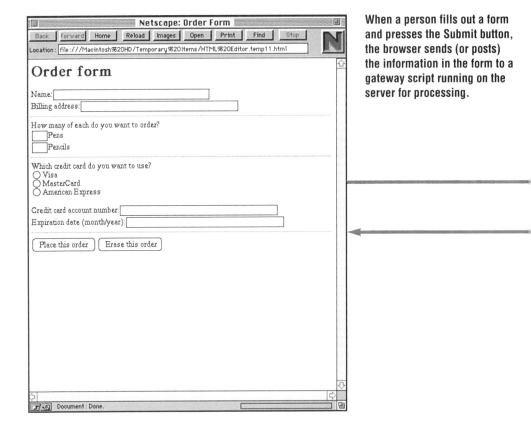

When a person fills out a form and presses the Submit button, the browser sends (or posts) the information in the form to a gateway script running on the server for processing.

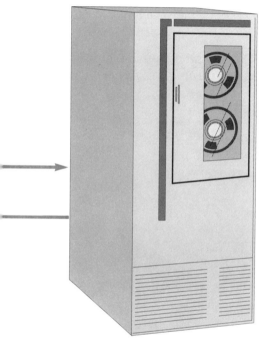

Information passed from the browser to the server gets processed by a gateway script. The processed information is sent back to the browser or forwarded to another location.

Basic Form Programming Elements

You must place a form inside the body of an HTML document. That means that every form has all the same tags required at the top and bottom of any other HTML document (see page 28).

Forms consist of three basic parts: the opening tag, the input types, and the submit button. The opening tag **<FORM>** defines the method by which the information gets to the gateway script and the name of the script itself. Input types, using the tag **<input type>**, include text fields, check boxes, radio buttons, and selection lists (see pages 76-83). The submit button **<input type=submit value="Submit">** is used to send the choices in the form to the gateway script. Additionally, a cancel button **<input type=reset value="Clear">** is used to clear or reset default choices in the form.

You can put more than one form in an HTML document and any number of input types within a single form. However, you cannot nest forms.

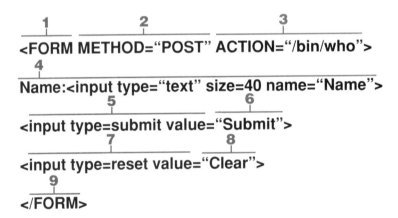

```
     1              2                    3
<FORM METHOD="POST" ACTION="/bin/who">
   4
Name:<input type="text" size=40 name="Name">
          5                      6
<input type=submit value="Submit">
            7                 8
<input type=reset value="Clear">
      9
</FORM>
```

1 Start the form with the <FORM> **tag**.

2 Use POST for the method of submitting the information to the gateway script.

3 Put the URL of the gateway script that you want to process the information between the quote marks as the action.

4 Put all the text and input types after the opening tag.

5 Put a submit button in your form to send the information to the gateway scripts.

6 Put the copy you want to appear in the submit button between the quote marks.

7 Put a reset button in your form to clear the form.

8 Put the copy that you want to appear in the reset button between the quote marks.

9 End every form with </FORM>.

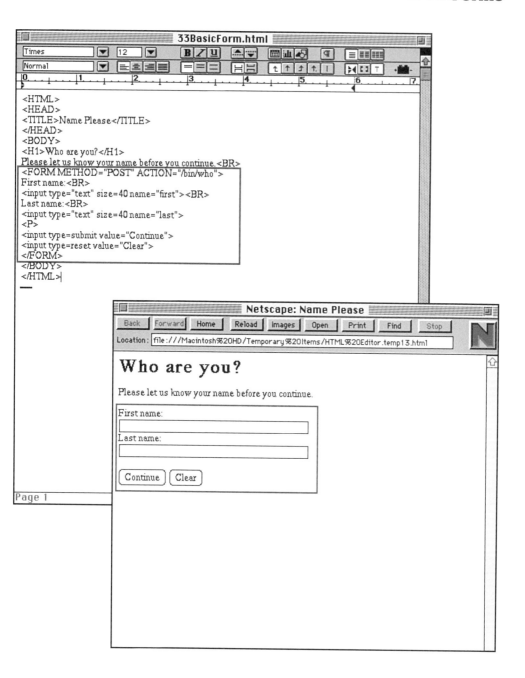

Text Fields

Text fields in forms enable a person to enter a word, phrase, or series of numbers. Text appears in the field when entered by the user. If you specify password as the input type instead of text, bullets hide anything entered from view.

You must include a size and name for each text field. Optional parameters include setting a maximum length for input and the default value of the field. The default value shows up in the field when the form first loads or when the reset button is pressed.

The browser sends the information in the field when the submit button in the form is clicked. It attaches the name to the information in the field as an identifier.

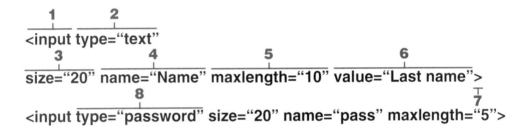

1 Start with the input tag `<input`.

2 Put text between the quote marks as the type of input.

3 Put the length of the text field you want between the quote marks as the size.

4 Put a label you want attached to this information between the quote marks as the name of input.

5 Put the maximum number of characters allowed in the field between the quote marks as the maxlength.

6 Put the copy you want to use as the default for the field between the quote marks as the value.

7 End with a closing `>` symbol.

8 Use password between the quote marks as the type if you want the input to appear as bullets on the screen.

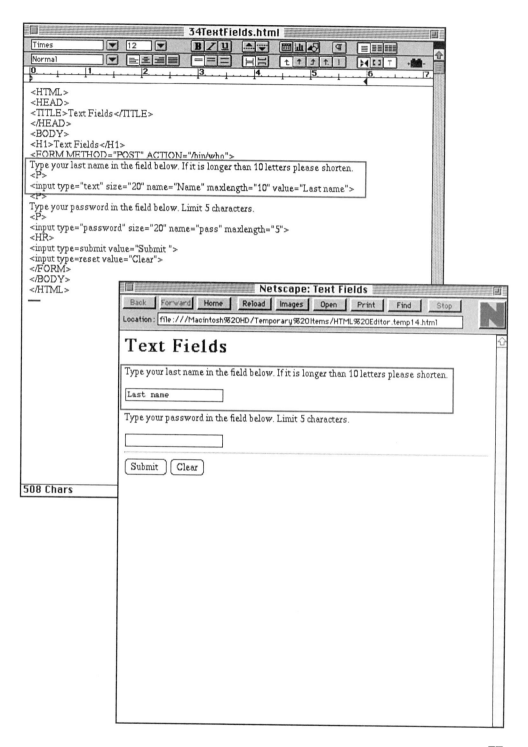

34TextFields.html

```
<HTML>
<HEAD>
<TITLE>Text Fields</TITLE>
</HEAD>
<BODY>
<H1>Text Fields</H1>
<FORM METHOD="POST" ACTION="/bin/who">
Type your last name in the field below. If it is longer than 10 letters please shorten.
<P>
<input type="text" size="20" name="Name" maxlength="10" value="Last name">
<P>
Type your password in the field below. Limit 5 characters.
<P>
<input type="password" size="20" name="pass" maxlength="5">
<HR>
<input type=submit value="Submit ">
<input type=reset value="Clear">
</FORM>
</BODY>
</HTML>
```

508 Chars

Netscape: Text Fields

Back | Forward | Home | Reload | Images | Open | Print | Find | Stop

Location: file:///Macintosh%20HD/Temporary%20Items/HTML%20Editor.temp14.html

Text Fields

Type your last name in the field below. If it is longer than 10 letters please shorten.

Last name

Type your password in the field below. Limit 5 characters.

Submit | Clear

Radio Buttons

Radio buttons allow a person to choose one item from a list. When you choose a radio button, the browser automatically deselects any other radio button you previously selected.

You must include a name and value for each radio button. The default selection shows up in the field when the form first loads or when the reset button is pressed. The browser sends the name and value for each radio button when the submit button in the form is clicked.

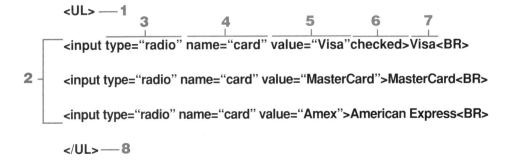

```
<UL> — 1
         3              4            5          6        7

  <input type="radio" name="card" value="Visa"checked>Visa<BR>

2 <input type="radio" name="card" value="MasterCard">MasterCard<BR>

  <input type="radio" name="card" value="Amex">American Express<BR>

  </UL> — 8
```

1 Start by creating a list.

2 Put the input tag in front of each radio button.

3 Type radio between the quote marks as the type of input.

4 Put the same text for the name between the quote marks for each radio button in the list.

5 Put the text you want attached to this selection between the quote marks as the value of radio button.

6 Set the default as selected by including the word checked.

7 Put the copy you want to appear next to the radio button after the closing > symbol.

8 End the list.

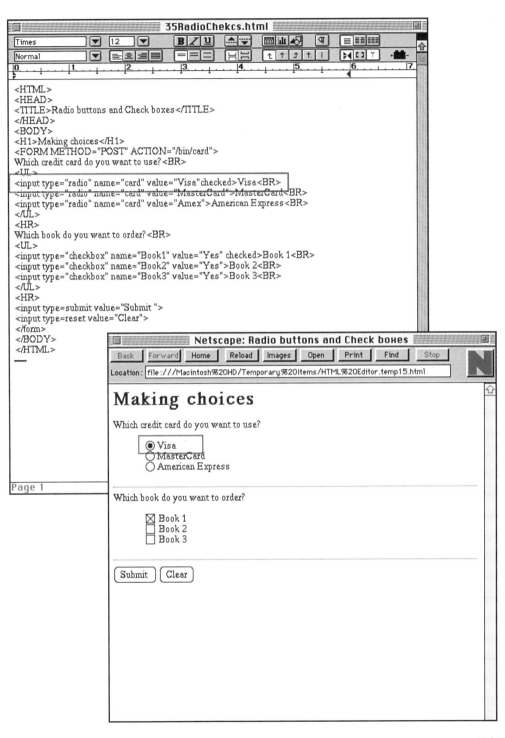

```
<HTML>
<HEAD>
<TITLE>Radio buttons and Check boxes</TITLE>
</HEAD>
<BODY>
<H1>Making choices</H1>
<FORM METHOD="POST" ACTION="/bin/card">
Which credit card do you want to use?<BR>
<UL>
<input type="radio" name="card" value="Visa"checked>Visa<BR>
<input type="radio" name="card" value="MasterCard">MasterCard<BR>
<input type="radio" name="card" value="Amex">American Express<BR>
</UL>
<HR>
Which book do you want to order?<BR>
<UL>
<input type="checkbox" name="Book1" value="Yes" checked>Book 1<BR>
<input type="checkbox" name="Book2" value="Yes">Book 2<BR>
<input type="checkbox" name="Book3" value="Yes">Book 3<BR>
</UL>
<HR>
<input type=submit value="Submit ">
<input type=reset value="Clear">
</form>
</BODY>
</HTML>
```

Page 1

35RadioChekcs.html

Times   12   Normal

Netscape: Radio buttons and Check boxes

Back | Forward | Home | Reload | Images | Open | Print | Find | Stop

Location: file:///Macintosh%20HD/Temporary%20Items/HTML%20Editor.temp15.html

Making choices

Which credit card do you want to use?

- ⦿ Visa
- ○ MasterCard
- ○ American Express

Which book do you want to order?

- ☒ Book 1
- ☐ Book 2
- ☐ Book 3

[Submit] [Clear]

Check Boxes

Check boxes allow a person to choose one or more items from a list. When you choose a check box, the browser leaves selected any other check boxes you previously selected.

You must include a name and value for each check box. The default selection shows up in the field when the form first loads or when the reset button is pressed. The browser sends the name and value for each check box when the submit button in the form is clicked.

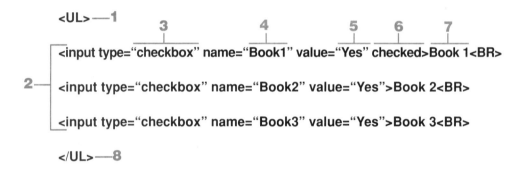

1. Start by creating a list.

2. Put the input tag in front of each check box.

3. Put checkbox between the quote marks as the type of input.

4. Put the different text for the name between the quote marks for each check box in the list.

5. Put the same text for the value between the quote marks for each check box in the list.

6. Set the default for each check box you want selected by including the word checked.

7. Put the copy you want to appear next to the check box after the closing > symbol.

8. End the list.

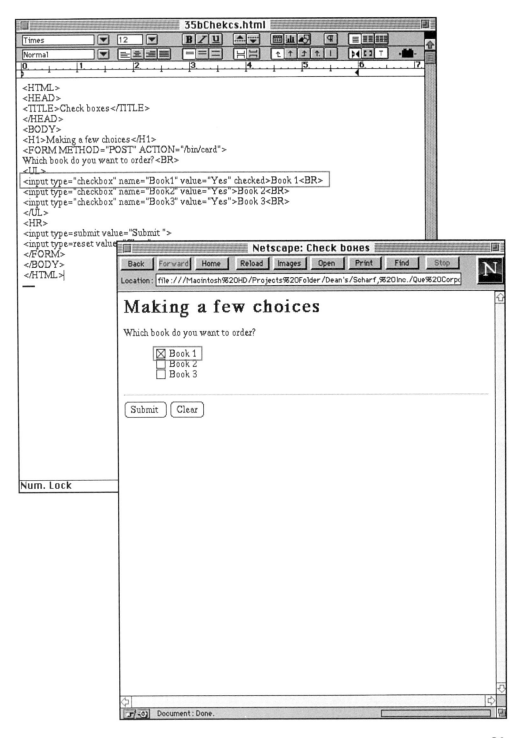

Selection Lists

HTML forms offer two more common methods of presenting predetermined choices in addition to radio buttons and check boxes. These are selection lists, better known as the pop-up menu, and scrolling lists.

Pop-up menus allow a person to choose only one item from a list just like radio buttons. The first option listed in the HTML document is the default selection when the form first loads or when the reset button is pressed. However, you can change the default to an item lower in the list by using the **selected** argument.

Scrolling lists allow a person to choose one or more items from a list. Options are not highlighted when the form first loads or when the reset button is pressed. However, you can set the default to highlight any item in the list by using the **selected** argument.

The text of each selected option serves as the value for pop-up menus and scrolling lists. The browser sends the name and value for each selected option when the submit button in the form is clicked.

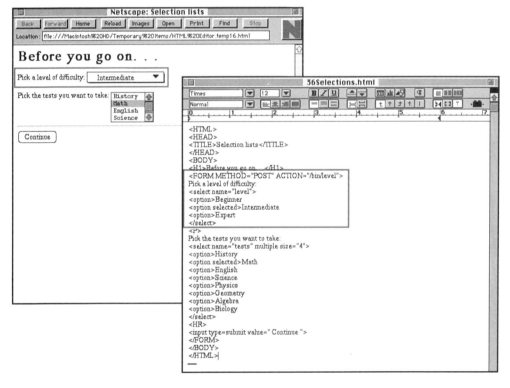

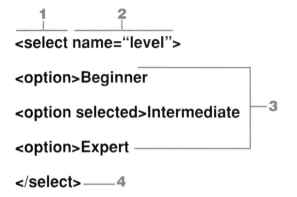

```
         1           2
<select name="level">

<option>Beginner

<option selected>Intermediate ──3

<option>Expert ──────────────

</select> ──4
```

1 Start with the selection tag.

2 Put the name of the pop-up menu between quote marks.

3 Put the option tag in front of the text of each item in the pop-up menu. Insert the word *selected* after option to change the default to an item lower in the list.

4 End with the select closing tag.

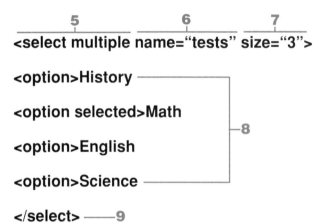

```
            5              6           7
<select multiple name="tests" size="3">

<option>History ──────────

<option selected>Math

<option>English          ──8

<option>Science ─────────

</select> ──9
```

5 Start with the selection tag. Include *multiple* for scrolling lists.

6 Put the name of the scrolling list between quote marks.

7 Put the depth of the scrolling list window between quote marks.

8 Put the option tag in front of the text of each item in the scrolling list. Insert the word *selected* after option to set the default to highlight any item in the list.

9 End with the select closing tag.

Home Pages

The first HTML document that you want people to see when they get to your Web site is called a *home page*. Home pages set the tone for the rest of your pages. Whether you design splashy or purely functional home pages, they should include certain elements.

Good home pages describe the service the page provides or tell the user what information is available. They instruct new users about unique features or software that is needed. They include an address for feedback. How you accomplish this is your decision.

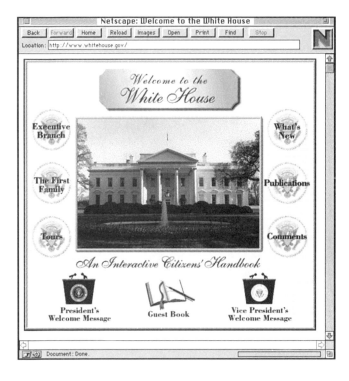

Splashy home pages have big graphics. Sometimes large image maps act as navigation for the document as a whole. Others have graphic navigation bars that repeat on every page. Remember, big graphics mean your home page will take a long time to transfer over the Web. A first-time user may cancel before the page ever loads.

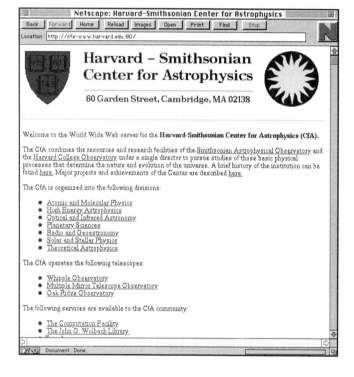

Table of contents-style home pages rely heavily on linked text. Sometimes small graphics accompany the text. Everyone knows how to use a table of contents, so there is no learning curve for this type of page. Using text exclusively means your home page will take the shortest time possible to transfer over the Web.

Structuring Multi-Page Documents— Linear

One way to present information is with a linear structure. A person moves forward or back just like turning pages in a book. One HTML file follows the next. Each HTML file includes a link to the next and preceding files. You determine the order in which the information is presented.

You do not need to make a diagram of linear documents; these documents do not have complicated connections to keep track of. Just remember to check the URLs in the links to the next and preceding files when you add or remove a file in the structure.

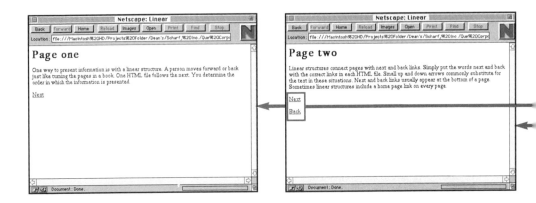

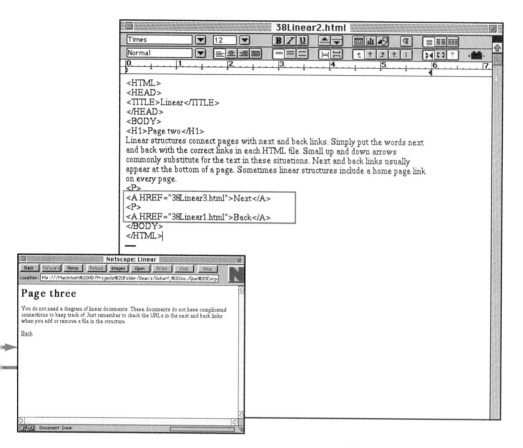

Linear structures connect pages with next and back links. Simply put the words "next" and "back" with the correct links in each HTML file. Small up and down arrows commonly substitute for the text in these situations. Next and back links usually appear at the bottom of a page. Sometimes linear structures include a home page link on every page.

Structuring Multi-Page Documents—Non-Linear

One way to present information is with a non-linear structure, in which a person jumps between inter-connected pages. One HTML file relates to many others like a three-dimensional maze. The person viewing your documents determines the order in which the information is presented from the possibilities you provide.

Non-linear structures connect pages with hypertext links. Simply put as many text and graphic links in each HTML file as you want. Home page links usually appear at the bottom of each page. Sometimes non-linear structures include linear sections.

Draw a diagram of non-linear documents. Even simple documents have many connections to keep track of. A diagram helps you keep track of all the files and links, making updates easier. When you remove pages, you're less likely to overlook important links if you have a good diagram.

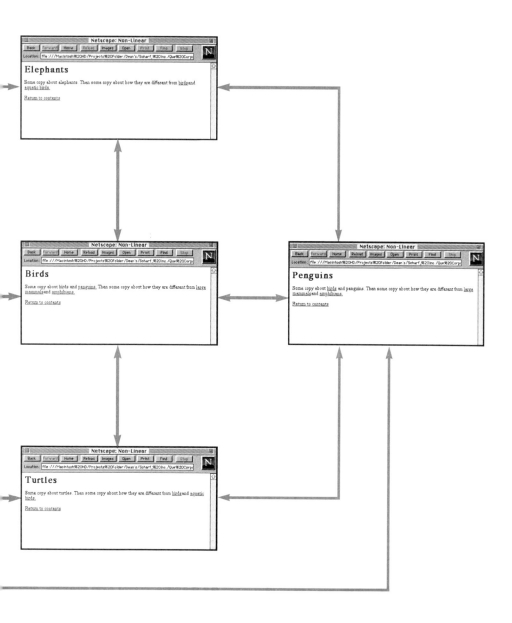

Navigation

Navigation within and between HTML files is important. If you provide good navigation, people will find it easy to use your service or purchase your products. Think about the basic mechanisms needed to get around the files, but also think about what makes them easier to use.

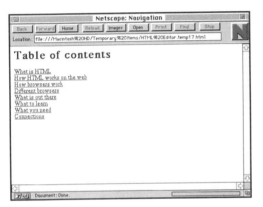

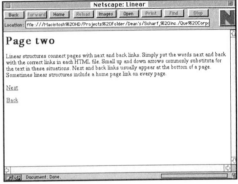

A table of contents is one of the most common means of navigation. Each item in the table of contents links to another HTML file or to an anchor in the same file. A person reads through the topics, jumps quickly to one of interest, and then returns to the contents.

Simple paging (or a linear structure, see page 86) takes little advantage of the hypertext capabilities of HTML. One HTML file follows the next just like the pages in a book. There are times when this makes good sense. For example, no one gets lost in a maze of information when paging.

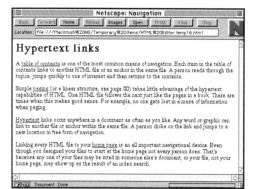

Hypertext links can occur anywhere in a document as often as you like. Any word or graphic can link to another file or anchor within the same file. A person clicks on the link and jumps to a new location in a free form of navigation.

Linking every HTML file to your home page is an all-important navigational device. Even though you designed your files to start at the home page, not every person will start there. That's because any one of your files may be cited in someone else's document, or your file, not your home page, may show up as the result of an index search.

Navigational Aids

People need help keeping track of where they are in the maze of information you can create with hypertext links. They also like Web documents to be easy to use. Some simple navigational aids can help on both accounts. These are in addition to basic navigation provided by things like a table of contents, simple paging, hypertext, and links to home pages, as discussed on the previous pages.

Clear headings help people know what they are looking at. When properly worded, headings concisely describe a file's content or function. Some headings describe how the current file relates to the whole document.

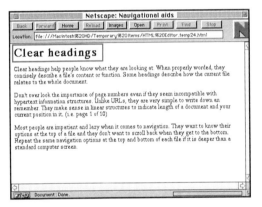

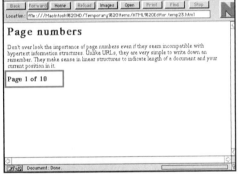

Clear, concise headings communicate quickly, allowing a person to decide whether to stop or go on.

Page numbers give a person a sense of place within a large document.

Don't overlook the importance of page numbers, even if they seem incompatible with hypertext information structures. Unlike URLs, page numbers are very simple to write down and remember. They make sense in linear structures to indicate the length of a document and your current position in it (i.e., page 1 of 10).

Most people are impatient and lazy when it comes to navigation. They want to know their options at the top of a file and they don't want to scroll back when they get to the bottom. Repeat the same navigation options at the top and bottom of each file if it is longer than a standard computer screen.

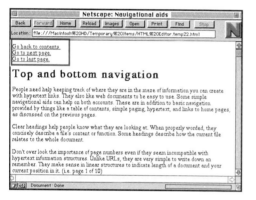

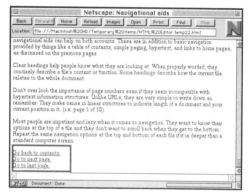

Navigation options at the top of a file avoid having to hunt for options within the text.

Navigation options at the bottom of a file provide logical next steps in the information flow.

Design Issues

Design on the Web means two things: structural information design and graphic design. The previous pages cover some basic structural design issues and suggest techniques for organizing the information. Other books go into greater depth than this book has space for.

When it comes to graphic design, electronic publishing with HTML is similar to desktop publishing. Software, however, does not make you a designer; if you know you are bad at design, don't try. Hire help. Stick with text. Keep it simple.

If you can design, knock yourself out. Remember that a few factors remain out of your control.

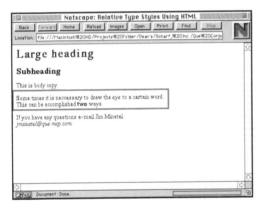

The available fonts and typestyle preferences on the user's computer can differ from those on your screen.

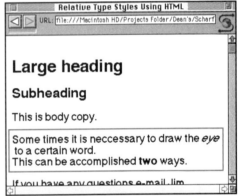

This is the same file as to the left viewed with different type preerences.

A rescaled browser window can crop graphics and rewrap text, causing different line breaks. Graphics meant to appear together on one line may stack instead.

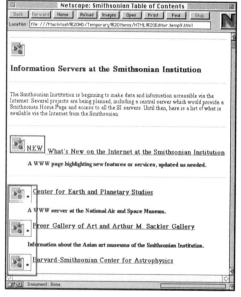

Long load times for those big graphics you spent hours on can cause people to cancel before they reach your page. Also, keep in mind that some people on the Web browse with the image loading turned off.

Beyond Design

The reason for any HTML document is the information, product, or service it provides. The text, graphics, sound, and video files all support that goal—they make it useful, easy, clear, and convenient. Sometimes the right text in the right place accomplishes this in a big way.

Include notes on external files. For FTP links, include file sizes. This helps the user estimate how long transfers will take. People can decide if they really want the file, and then decide when to schedule a download and how to make room on their hard disk. For sound and video, include the format and file size (see page 66).

Date your file in the text, just like newspapers or letters, so that people can tell at-a-glance if they've already read the file. Or, include a what's new page for each update.

Leave behind a pointer page when you change your URL. It is just like getting a recorded message when someone changes their phone number. Pointer pages don't have to be pretty, just effective.

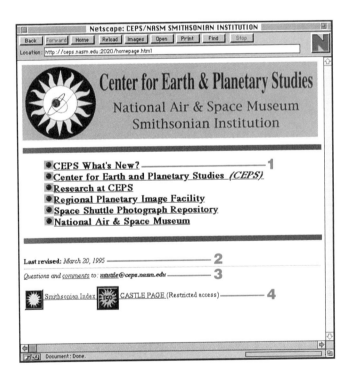

1 A "what's new" link gives people a quick way of skimming the current document highlights.

2 Dating the file in the text tells people at-a-glance if they have read it already.

3 E-mail links are a convenient feature in some browsers.

4 Notes that tell of restricted access or FTP file sizes help the user to avoid wasting time.

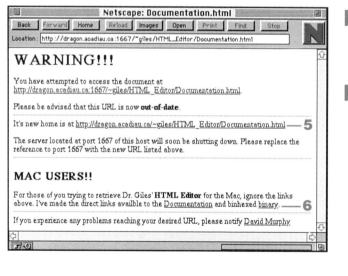

5 At the old address, provide the new address along with any important messages.

6 Include links to URLs that people expect to find, as well as related URLs.

Comments in Programming

You can insert lines of text in your HTML files that browsers will not display; these are called *comments*. Comments allow you to annotate your HTML programming so that your notes remain a part of the file itself. Every line of a comment begins with the **<!** tag and ends with the **>** tag. Do not use any other tags inside comments, as these will confuse some browsers that display the comment instead of ignoring it.

Use a comment when you want to remember something special about your file, for example, why you used certain URLs or gateway scripts.

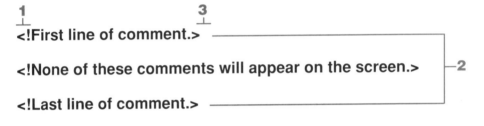

<!First line of comment.>

<!None of these comments will appear on the screen.>

<!Last line of comment.>

1 Start by placing the opening <! tag in front of the comment.

2 Put every line of comment between its own comment tags.

3 End with a closing > symbol after every line of comment.

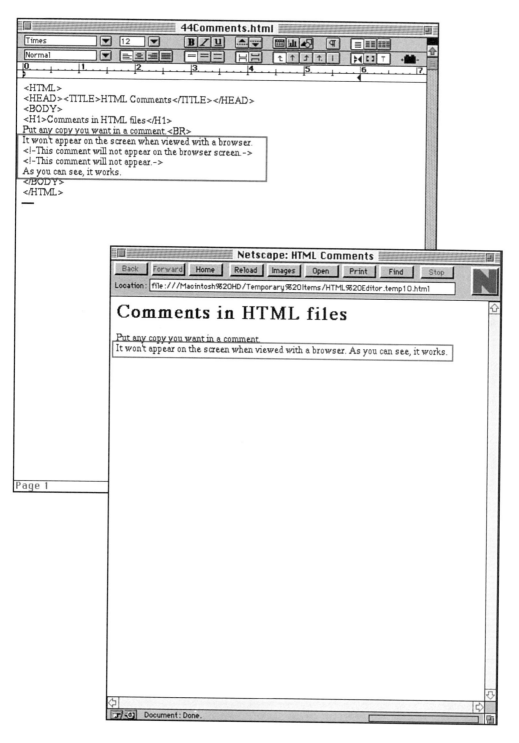

Consistency in Programming

You want to format HTML word processing files in a consistent and logical way for your own benefit, not for the browser's. Browsers don't notice how you format your files, they only notice the tags. They ignore extra returns and spaces unless you tag the copy as preformatted text (see page 64).

Whether you type one continuous line of code or put a return after every word, both documents will look the same when browsed as long as the content is identical.

Whenever possible, format the file so that it mimics the look of the browsed file. This makes it easier to visualize the browser page and find mistakes. Isolate key elements on separate lines so that you can check them at a glance. Find a consistent way of formatting files that makes sense to you and stick with it.

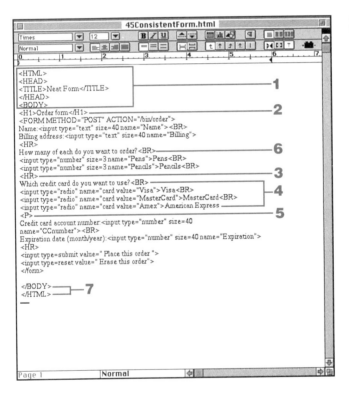

1 Put each tag in the HTML header at the top on a line of its own.

2 Put elements like headings on lines of their own.

3 Put rules on their own lines.

4 Use the identical order for arguments of each radio button, check box, and selection list. Put every item on its own line.

5 Put paragraph breaks on their own line so that they look like the line space they create.

6 Put line breaks at the end of the line where they perform their functions.

7 Put each tag in the HTML footer at the bottom on a line of its own.

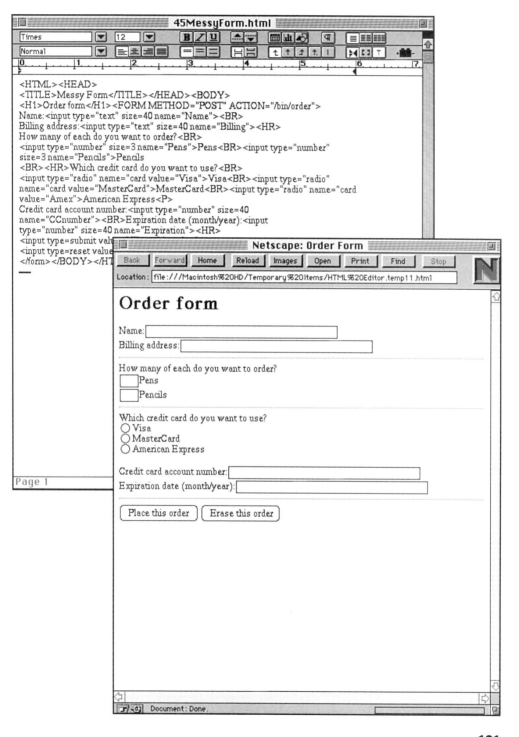

Testing

Before posting any pages, you have to test them. Programming is inherently buggy even when it is as simple as HTML. You should test your files locally and keep them all on your own hard disk off any network before you post them on the Web. View them with several different browsers, not just your favorite one. You will discover differences that may be important enough to warrant changes.

Besides the obvious examples on the next page, make sure you check the following list. Keep in mind, though, that many of these items will be difficult—if not impossible—to check until the HTML files are posted on the Web server. You can arrange to post pages that require a password for viewing so that you can test everything before it is made public.

- *Spelling.* Spell check the file or ask someone else to proofread the screen for you.

- *Navigation.* Make sure every page has the necessary navigation and that it works correctly.

- *External files.* Place graphic, sound, and video files where they can be found and loaded. Include alternate text for non-graphical browsers.

- *Load times.* Are they acceptable or are they too long?

- *Forms.* Do the gateway scripts work properly?

- *Dummy test.* Have someone new to the document run through it; something is bound to turn up that you never noticed.

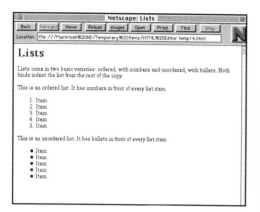

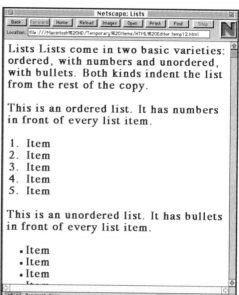

In this example, a missing closing tag for a heading drastically changed the look of the browsed file. The heading style remained in effect for the rest of the text.

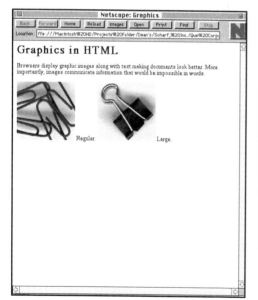

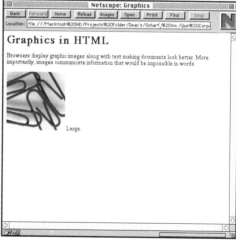

In this example, a misplaced graphic file or incorrect URL stopped the browser from loading one image.

Authoring with HTML Editor 1.0 for the Macintosh

HTML Editor 1.0 is a simple, uncluttered, point-and-click authoring tool for the Macintosh. It automates the most repetitive typing tasks that accompany HTML programming, keeping the typing to a minimum. The pop-up menus and buttons at the top of the window perform these functions for you.

The software is essentially a simple word processor that writes text-only files. It has the capability of displaying coded elements, like links and headings, in different text styles and colors to help you troubleshoot files.

You can get documentation for HTML Editor 1.0 on the Web at **http://drag-on.acadiau.ca/~giles/HTML_Editor/Documentation.html**, or you can get the software at **FTP://cs.dal.ca/giles/HTML_Editor_1.0.sit.hqx**.

HTML Editor 1.0 is also included with *Special Edition Using HTML* on HTMLCD, a Windows, Mac, and UNIX CD-ROM that accompanies the book.

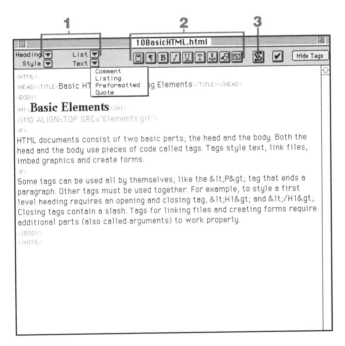

1 Pop-up menus insert tags for standard code strings.

2 A series of buttons inserts tags or brings up dialog boxes for locating linked files.

3 You can launch a browser from the editor to view the HTML file.

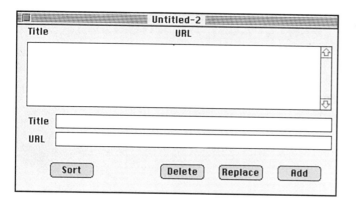

A window for storing frequently used URLs is available.

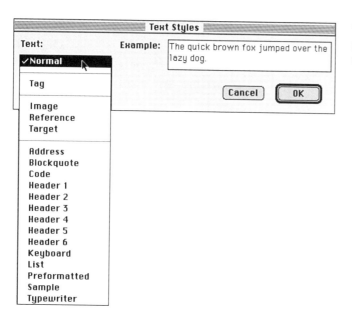

You can customize the font and color of text as it is displayed within HTML Editor.

Authoring with HTML.Edit for the Macintosh

HTML.Edit is a full-featured authoring tool for the Macintosh. It automates almost every aspect of writing HTML files. You can import text or type it in directly. Pop-up menus on a floating palette insert tags, and dialog boxes manage other common tasks. Some dialog boxes index files, URLs, graphics, and so on. You add, delete, or edit as you work. You can even pick and choose the ones you need when you're creating a new file.

The software is a hypercard stand-alone application. Each document you create becomes part of the software itself. Export documents when you need text-only HTML files separate from the software.

You can get documentation for HTML.Edit on the Web at **http://nctn.oact. hq.nasa.gov/tools/HTMLedit/HTMLedit.html** or you can get the software at **/ftp://ftp.hawaii/edu/mirrors/info-mac/TextProcessing/ HTML/html-edit-15b1.hqx**.

HTML.Edit is also included with *Special Edition Using HTML* on HTMLCD, a Windows, Mac, and UNIX CD-ROM that accompanies the book.

1 Type the header for your document in this area. A pop-up menu allows you to choose from headers that you define in a special window.

2 Type the body of your document in this area.

3 Type the footer for your document here. A pop-up menu allows you to choose from footers that you define in a special window.

4 A floating palette enables you to insert tags or bring up dialog boxes for locating linked files.

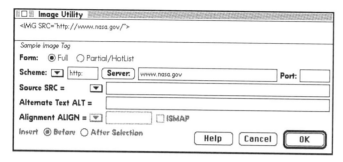

Various windows like this
image utility dialog box speed
your work through pop-up
menus you include frequently
used graphics.

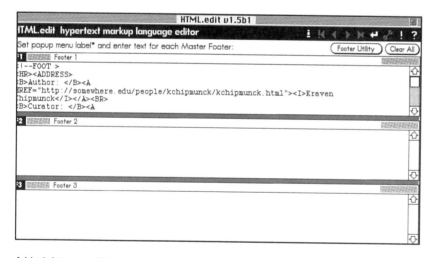

Add, delete, or edit footers
through this window. Each one
is available through a pop-up
menu when creating a document in the software.

Authoring with SoftQuad's HoTMetaL in UNIX

HoTMetaL was one of the original semi-WYSIWYG HTML editors available for UNIX machines. It is capable of displaying many of the attributes of text such as font type and size, while at the same time displaying HTML tags as distinctive icons. The program has gotten so popular among Web page authors that SoftQuad has also developed an MS Windows version, and is considering Mac and PowerMac versions as well.

HoTMetaL eases the burden of having to memorize the exact language of HTML, and completely eliminates the need to actually type the HTML tags yourself. Inserting tags is simple; you highlight a section of text, choose Insert Tag from the Markup menu, and select the appropriate HTML command from a scrolling list. HoTMetaL automatically inserts the tags and changes the fonts appropriately. When you are finished with the document, HoTMetaL will generate the HTML file and save it to disk.

HoTMetaL is available in two "levels": shareware and commercial (dubbed HoTMetaL PRO). The shareware version is free to download and install to generate Web pages immediately. If you like it, you are encouraged to purchase the commercial version, which includes a spell checker, thesaurus, and an "HTML Verifier," which automatically validates the HTML code in your Web pages. To try it out for yourself, point your Web browser to **http://www.sq.com/** and follow the links.

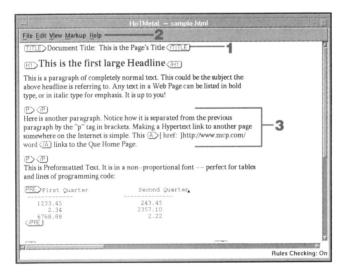

1 HoTMetaL is an X Windows application, so it can easily combine textual and graphical elements in the same application window.

2 Pull-down menus provide access to HTML tags and commands.

3 HoTMetaL mimics the style of Web pages while creating them, yet displays the HTML tags directly, so that you always know what commands are being used.

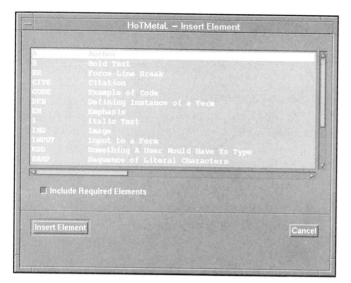

The Insert Element dialog box makes it easy to make simple changes in style, or use more complex, data-oriented HTML commands for your Web page.

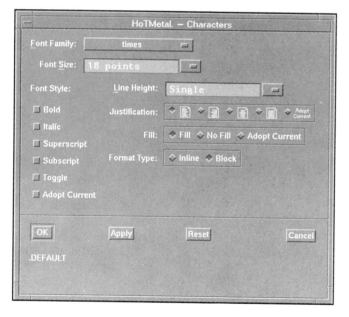

The Characters dialog box allows you to change the display font—perfect for seeing how your Web pages look in different browsers using different fonts.

Authoring HTML with html-helper-mode in UNIX

True UNIX-heads work at the text-based command line, many of them say, and their tool of choice is EMACS. EMACS is a programmable text editor/command shell/file utility that, when mastered, may be the only program you'll ever need. EMACS is available for free and is installed on most UNIX systems, so you can start using it right away. html-helper-mode (h-h-m) is a free module that plugs into EMACS, turning it into a powerful Web page generator in addition to everything else it does.

h-h-m is essentially a thorough macro set for EMACS, reducing even the most complicated HTML commands into a series of keypresses. Whether or not these keypresses are easier to remember than the HTML commands themselves is subject to debate, but if you're already into EMACS, you will get used to h-h-m very quickly.

h-h-m is available directly from its author at **http://www.santafe.edu/ ~nelson/tools/**. By jumping to it, you can retrieve h-h-m, some help and installation files, and even EMACS itself if you don't yet have it. While not as elegant as other graphical HTML editors, if you are working at a text-only UNIX terminal, it really is the best alternative to writing raw HTML files.

1 EMACS and html-helper-mode are text-mode applications, making them quick and responsive even on older or overburdened UNIX machines.

2 A complete online help system is available by typing Ctrl+h, b (that's Control+h followed by a "b" all by itself).

3 h-h-m displays the HTML tags directly alongside the text of your Web page—certainly *not* WYSIWYG, but there's never any question about what tags are in use.

111

Authoring with Microsoft Internet Assistant/Word for Windows

Internet Assistant is a comprehensive module that "plugs in" to Word for Win-dows 6.0a or greater, transforming the popular word processor into *both* a powerful HTML file creator and a robust Web browser program similar to Netscape or Mosaic.

Because Word is a WYSIWYG word processor, emphasized words are in italics, links are underlined and colored blue, and inline images appear alongside text. You can also activate the Internet Assistant's Browser mode and view the actual HTML file as a browser would display the file (because the browser mode is a full-fledged Web browser).

Perhaps the best thing about the Internet Assistant is it is completely free to all registered users of Word for Windows (procrastinators who haven't filled out their registration cards can use it too). You can retrieve it on the Web by jumping to **http://www.microsoft.com/** and following the links, or you can get it directly from **ftp://ftp.microsoft.com/deskapps/word/ winword-public/ia/wordia.exe**.

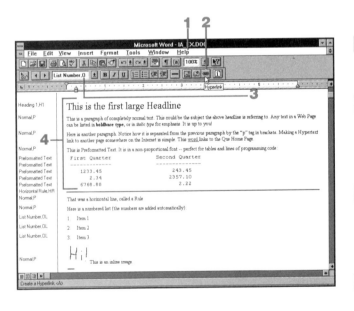

1 Completely customized pull-down menus make inserting HTML tags easier.

2 Buttons for quick access to HTML commands and browsing tools are automatically inserted into the Word toolbars.

3 The Styles drop-down list provides access to most paragraph-level HTML tags, such as preformatted text, header levels 1-6, and lists.

4 While the HTML tags themselves aren't visible, the Internet Assistant mimics the appearance of finished Web pages as you write them.

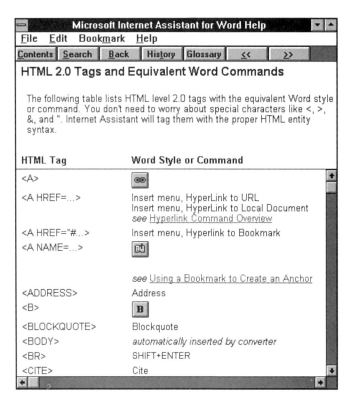

As a bonus, an extensive HTML command listing is provided in a thorough Hypertext Windows help file.

Unlike many other Word add-on programs, the Internet Assistant makes it easy to insert HTML tags not already built into the pull-down menus with a simple dialog box.

113

Authoring HTML with CU_HTML in Windows

CU_HTML is probably the best of the noncommercial Word for Windows HTML templates you could use. While not as ambitious in scope as Microsoft's Internet Assistant, it doesn't fundamentally alter how WinWord works, plus it works just fine with Word for Windows 2.0.

CU_HTML (which stands for the Chinese University in Hong Kong) is a set of macros hooked into a single toolbar and pull-down menu, combined with a document template, that is capable of displaying a Web page in near-WYSIWYG format. As you write your page, you assign paragraph styles with the Style menu and other commands through the toolbar, so there's no need to memorize complex HTML tags. CU_HTML only supports a basic set of HTML tags and inline images, so you won't be able to create online forms or perform other special effects—but for most casual Web page authors, this isn't a problem. CU_HTML makes it especially easy to transform existing Word documents into attractive Web pages.

CU_HTML is available directly from its authors at **http://www.cuhk. hk/csc/cu_html/cu_html.htm**, though most major anonymous FTP sites also have this relatively small file. If you're just beginning to spread your Web page-authoring wings, you can't go wrong with CU_HTML.

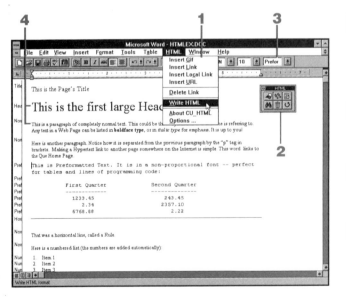

1 CU_HTML adds a single, unobtrusive menu to WinWord's menu bar, which appears only when you are writing Web pages.

2 A small, powerful toolbar provides quick access to most major HTML commands.

3 Use the Style menu to assign paragraph-level HTML commands to text.

4 Your Web page is displayed with different sized fonts and inline images as you write it.

CU_HTML will automatically build links to Web pages using the *.HTML file extension (the UNIX Web page server standard extension) instead of DOS *.HTM extensions from the Options dialog box.

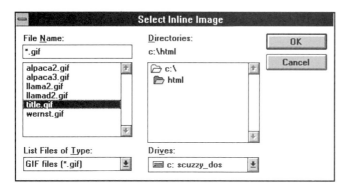

Inserting an inline image is as simple as opening a file in Windows.

115

Authoring with SoftQuad's HoTMetaL in MS Windows

HoTMetaL was one of the original semi-WYSIWYG HTML editors available for UNIX machines, and it became so popular that a Windows version was soon written. This new version is getting so popular that it has been getting new features faster than the UNIX version, so Windows users are really benefiting from this arrangement. While writing Web pages, HoTMetal is capable of displaying many of the attributes of text such as font type and size along with inline images, while at the same time displaying HTML tags as distinctive icons. In this manner, the program is suitable for knowledgeable beginners and experts alike.

HoTMetaL eases the burden of memorizing the exact language of HTML, and completely eliminates the need to actually type the HTML tags yourself. Inserting tags is simple; you simply highlight a section of text, choose Insert Tag from the Markup menu, and select the appropriate HTML command from a scrolling list. HoTMetaL automatically inserts the tags and changes the fonts appropriately. When you are finished with the document, HoTMetaL will generate the HTML file and save it to disk. Additionally, it can "validate" the HTML file, ensuring that all the HTML commands have been used correctly—a real benefit, plus it can automatically load the HTML file you are working on into your Web browser at any time, enabling you to see how it will *really* look.

HoTMetaL is available in two "levels": shareware and commercial (dubbed HoTMetaL PRO). The shareware version is free to download and install so that you can generate Web pages immediately. If you like it, you are encouraged to purchase the commercial version, which includes a spell checker and thesaurus. To try it out for yourself, point your Web browser to **http://www.sq.com/** and follow the links.

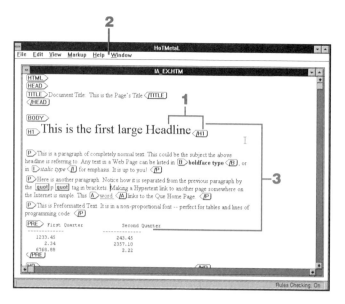

1 HoTMetaL combines the visible HTML tags of advanced HTML editors with the different fonts and visible inline images of the beginner programs.

2 Pull-down menus provide access to HTML tags and commands.

3 HoTMetaL mimics the style of Web pages while creating them, yet displays the HTML tags directly, so you always know what commands are being used.

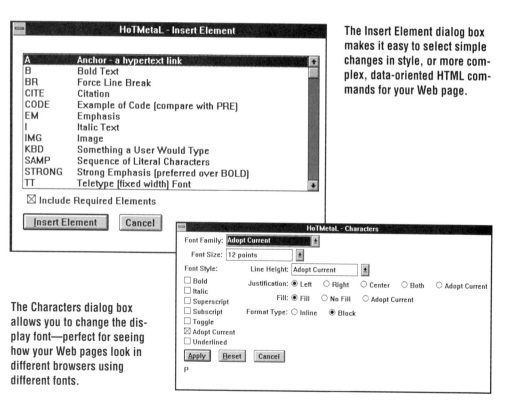

The Insert Element dialog box makes it easy to select simple changes in style, or more complex, data-oriented HTML commands for your Web page.

The Characters dialog box allows you to change the display font—perfect for seeing how your Web pages look in different browsers using different fonts.

Authoring with HTML Assistant in MS Windows

HTML Assistant was one of the first Windows-based HTML editors available, and it has matured nicely. While it is not a WYSIWYG editor, it is simple to install and use, and it can actually grow with you as your HTML writing skills improve: you can add new or advanced HTML commands to the toolbar with relative ease. It can also automatically load the HTML file you are working on into any Web browser you designate (it works especially well with Cello in this respect), so its lack of special fonts is not a big problem.

While HTML Assistant assumes you know how to use HTML tags, it places them within the program's toolbar so you do not need to memorize exactly how to write them. HTML Assistant also excels at reading the bookmark files of Mosaic and Cello (and Netscape in the future), and copying the URLs it finds into the Web page you are designing. If the thought of retyping dozens of accumulated URLs makes you want to take an aspirin, this feature will make your HTML authoring experience much less painful.

HTML Assistant is available as a shareware version and as the commercial "HTML Assistant PRO" version, which permits the editing of large files and includes an HTML "Wizard," which automates much of the Web page authoring process. To check out the free version, point your Web browser to **http://cs.dal.ca/ftp/htmlasst/htmlafaq.html**.

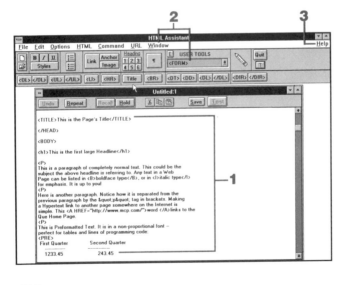

1 HTML Assistant displays your work in a single font (including the HTML tags themselves), which makes the program quick even on slower machines.

2 Pull-down menus and toolbar buttons provide access to HTML tags and commands.

3 A very complete context-sensitive, hypertext Help file is always just a click away—many HTML editors lack this vital feature.

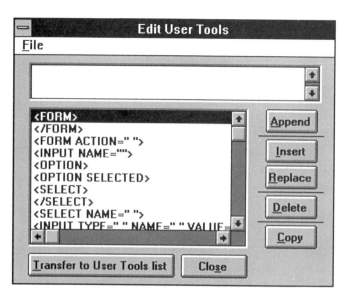

The User Tools dialog box makes it easy to add new HTML commands to the toolbar.

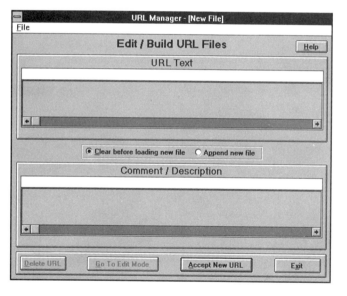

The URL Manager dialog box allows you to easily add complex URLs stored in your Web browser's bookmark files to your Web page—no retyping necessary!

Posting Pages

No one will see your HTML files unless you post them (make them accessible) on a server in a network.

You can post files on a server in a closed network, like one at work, if you want to restrict viewing to people in that network. Or, you can make your HTML documents available to everyone browsing the Web by placing them on an Internet server. Some Internet servers also restrict access to files. For example, you may have to subscribe or obtain special clearance.

Send your HTML, graphic, sound, and video files along with any gateway scripts to the server. You can do this over the Internet or by sending a disk to the server administrator. Use the method the administrator prefers.

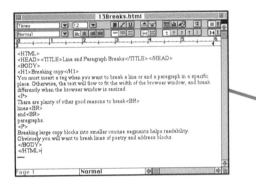

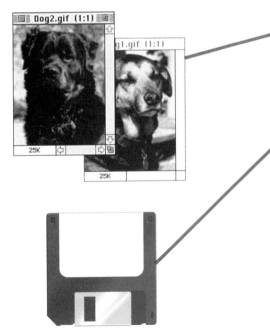

The people operating the server you work with govern how you post pages to the server. If they like do-it-yourselfers and your files are small, you can probably transfer them over the Internet. Otherwise, you just send a disk and the system administrator does the rest. It's a very good idea to recheck all of the links, scripts, etc. to be sure they all work as soon as the pages are posted.

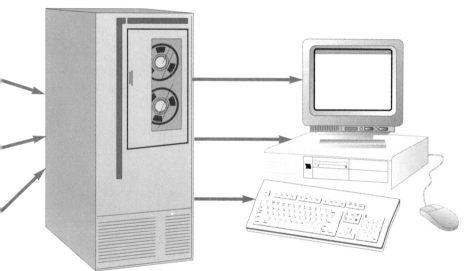

The server holds all your files and gateway scripts on a hard disk and makes the files available to Web browsers. It runs your gateway scripts and returns the results. Internet servers make files available over the high-speed data lines to other Internet servers and to computers with modems over dial-up connections.

Many individuals browsing the Web can view your HTML documents at the same time when they are placed on an Internet server. Each computer requests a file from the server by using its URL address.

Finding a Server

New Internet servers are popping up all over; you don't have to look very hard to find one these days. Most large corporations, government agencies, research institutes, and colleges and universities have servers. If not, they are most likely planning to set one up in the near future.

Check for a server where you work or study before you search for a commercial server for your files. It could be available to you free of charge. Ask the network administrator if you can use it.

To find a commercial server, start by asking friends and colleagues. Someone you know probably researched the topic recently and can save you time. If not, surf the Web and look for e-mail addresses of the commercial servers. See page 128 for a short list that can get you started.

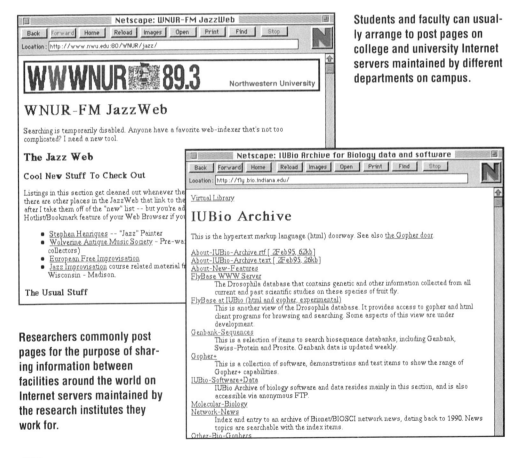

Students and faculty can usually arrange to post pages on college and university Internet servers maintained by different departments on campus.

Researchers commonly post pages for the purpose of sharing information between facilities around the world on Internet servers maintained by the research institutes they work for.

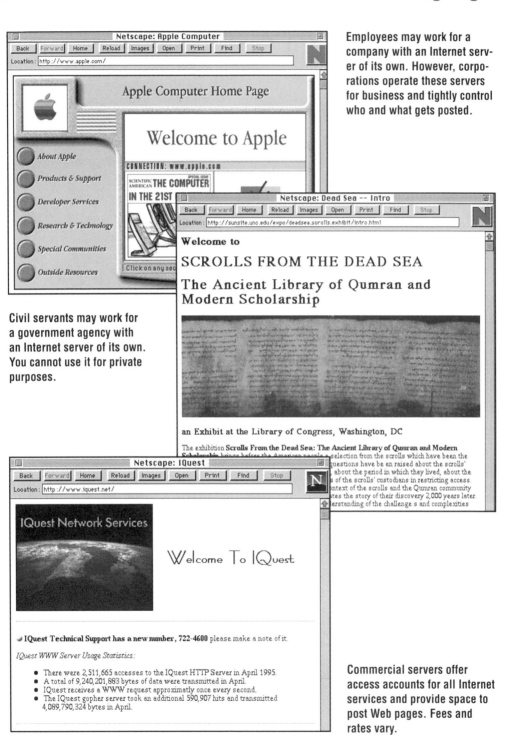

Employees may work for a company with an Internet server of its own. However, corporations operate these servers for business and tightly control who and what gets posted.

Civil servants may work for a government agency with an Internet server of its own. You cannot use it for private purposes.

Commercial servers offer access accounts for all Internet services and provide space to post Web pages. Fees and rates vary.

Should You Set Up Your Own Server?

In the past, setting up an Internet server has been a big undertaking. The hardware and software were complex and required significant technical expertise. They also cost a lot of money.

It's no longer true that a server will be prohibitively expensive. Relatively inexpensive all-in-one Web servers are now available that come bundled with hardware and software. But, don't underestimate the money required to connect to the Internet with a dedicated line.

Generally, individuals and small businesses have not considered setting up a server, it has been just as easy to rent space from a commercial server. However, many individuals are now setting up servers due to dropping costs.

Groups that should consider setting up a server include the organizations that you see on the Web already: corporations, schools, museums, and research institutes. They tend to be large and have equally large capital expenditure budgets for computer equipment each year. Commercial enterprises that expect significant income from Web services should consider setting up a server.

Are you considering setting up your own server? If your answers to these questions have more nos than yeses, consider space on a commercial server instead of setting up your own.

Historically, servers operated on a UNIX system had full-time system administrators. Recently, there's been a flood of PC and Macintosh software for this. There are several servers individuals might use for Windows for a simple Web site. Windows NT is fast becoming the platform of choice for new Web servers in corporate settings.

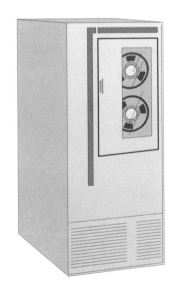

	Yes	No
Is Web publishing the best way to distribute your information?	☐	☐
Is a server part of a long-range strategy for your organization?	☐	☐
Do you need control of the server by your organization for security reasons?	☐	☐
Do you have the equipment and software already?	☐	☐
Do you have the know-how to set up and maintain a server?	☐	☐
Do you have the time it takes to be a system administrator or do you have a full-time system administrator on staff?	☐	☐
Can you afford to hire a full-time system administrator?	☐	☐
Do you need to have a programmer for the server you set up?	☐	☐
Can you program or do you have a programmer for the UNIX platform?	☐	☐
Do you have or can you afford a high-speed connection to the Internet?	☐	☐
Do you know all the costs involved?	☐	☐
Can you afford all the costs involved?	☐	☐

Setting Up Your Own Server

Once you decide to set up your own server, you need to design a system that meets your needs. There are more and more companies that sell out-of-the-box hardware and software systems at affordable prices. Sales representatives are eager to help.

Local telephone companies provide connections to the Internet. They sell or rent equipment that interfaces their line with your network. Shop around; your local baby bell isn't usually the cheapest source. T1 lines are the most common connections. They are reasonably fast for the money. An ISDN line provides an inexpensive alternative if you use the line for a part of the day and don't expect a high volume of traffic. You pay a monthly fee for the line and a rate for timed usage.

If you are interested in running a simple server for yourself or a small company, you should look at the book *Running a Perfect Web Site* by David Chandler. It includes a CD-ROM with server software for several platforms.

Ask yourself these questions:

- Do you just want a Web server or a full-featured Internet server that includes other Internet services, like e-mail and Gopher? You can get a cheap e-mail account at a local access provider rather than setting up a mail server of your own.

- Do you need to transact business or is it purely an information server? Secure systems cost more.

- How fast a transmission line do you need? Higher speed equals higher cost.

- What platform should you operate? Choose one that makes sense in your LAN.

A server begins the list of equipment you need. You will want to get a fast one with expandable memory and the capability of attaching multiple hard disks. You may also need a *router,* which manages the flow of data from other nodes on the Internet. It receives packets of information from other servers, reads the URLs, and sends them on to their destinations.

A system administrator will set up the server, maintain it, update software, troubleshoot problems, and manage file transfers.

127

Short List of Commercial Servers

There are hundreds, perhaps thousands, of companies selling their services as commercial Web servers. Here are just a few of them. Most of these servers are large national service providers. You may also find local providers in your area. Some of these providers also provide their services as Web authors and designers if you need to outsource that work, too.

Server	URL
Atlantic	http://www.atlantic.com/
Aztec Internet Services	http://www.aztec.com/pub/aztec/
Branch Information Services	http://branch.com/
Catalog.Com	http://www.catalog.com/catalog/top.html
CERFnet	http://www.cerfnet.com/cerfnet/services/ce rfnweb.html
CommerceNet CyberGate Inc.	http://www.commerce.net/
Cybersight Services	http://cybersight.com/cgi-bin/imi/s?main.gmml
Digital Marketing Inc.	http://www.digimark.net/
Digital Planet	http://www.digiplanet.com/DP/
Downtown Anywhere	http://www.awa.com/
EarthLink Network	http://www.earthlink.net/Other_svc.html
ElectriCiti	http://www.electriciti.com/
Electric Press Inc.	http://www.elpress.com/
Great Lakes Area Commercial Internet	http://www.glaci.com/info/aboutglaci.html
Home Pages Inc.	http://www.homepages.com/
Internet Distribution Services	http://www.service.com/
The Internet Group	http://www.tig.com/
Internet Information Services Inc.	http://www.iis.com/
Internet Information Systems	http://www.internet-is.com/
Internet Presence and Publishing	http://www.ip.net/

Server	URL
Internet Services Corporation	http://www.netservices.com/
InterNex Information Services	http://www.internex.net/homepage.html
Iquest Network Services	http://www.iquest.net/cw/hosting.html
MarketPlace.com	http://marketplace.com/
Net+Effects	http://www.net.effects.com:8080/ net-effects/infonow_server.html
NetCenter	http://netcenter.com/yellows/ advertisers.html
NETCOM	http://www.netcom.com/netcom/ prodserv. html
NetMarket	http://netmarket.com/nm/pages/home
New Jersey Computer Connection	http://www.njcc.com/services.html
New Media Publishing	http://www.melvin.com/WebLot/
The Pipeline	http://www.pipeline.com/business.html
Primenet	http://www.primenet.com/commercial/
PSINet	http://www.psi.net/orgservices/psiweb/
QuakeNet	http://www.quake.net/QuakeNet/ quakenet_web.html
Quantum Networking Solutions	http://www.gcr.com
The SEAMLESS WEBSite	http://seamless.com/chambers.html
The Sphere	http://www.thesphere.com/Sphere/ SphereO verview.html
SSNet	http://ssnet.com/ssnet/www.html
Stelcom	http://webscope.com/
Streams Online Media Development	http://streams.com/
Televisions Inc.	http://www.tvisions.com/
The Tenagra Corporation	http://arganet.tenagra.com/
TurnPike Metropolis †	http://turnpike.net/turnpike/metro.html
Virtual Broadcast Network	http://www.solutionsrc.com/
World Wide Access	http://www.wwa.com/wwa.html
XOR Network Engineering	http://plaza.xor.com/plaza/index.html
Z-Depth	http://www.zdepth.com/

† *Provides free space for non-commercial use*

Costs

Servers are definitely in business to make money. They do this through service fees, monthly rates, and commissions. Charges vary widely from server to server. You will not necessarily encounter all three costs at every server. Call a few to compare pricing and ask a lot of questions. Try to negotiate a better deal, if you can.

Large servers offer turnkey solutions. Staff programmers and designers do everything for you. You can also hire freelance programmers and designers at reasonable hourly rates.

Most servers charge setup fees when you first post your pages. It can involve programming that enables the server to track usage and generate reports. The reports tell you how many people look at which pages each month. Additional fees are charged for any work that you ask the server to do for you like programming or screen design.

Servers charge monthly rates for keeping your files posted. Some ask you to commit for a three month minimum to start. They base rates on the megabytes of hard disk space you require and the megabytes viewed per month. If you are in a retail business, you can find a server that processes credit cards for a fixed rate.

Some servers have lower fees and rates but get a commission on the sale of your products in a type of partnership. Their profits rise with yours. They may charge as much as 10% of gross sales for posting your pages, taking orders over the Net, and forwarding them to your fulfillment facility. They get paid whether you get your money from the customer or not.

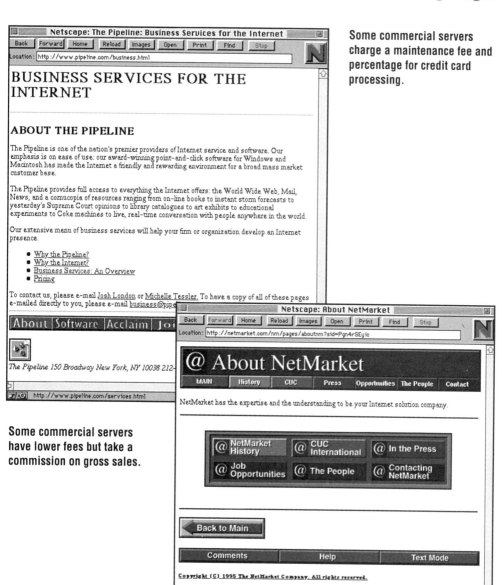

Some commercial servers charge a maintenance fee and percentage for credit card processing.

Some commercial servers have lower fees but take a commission on gross sales.

Check-Ups and Updates

You should check your posted documents over the Web periodically. Make sure the files are found at the URL you publicize, that they work correctly, and that the information is still up-to-date.

Things can go wrong over time as system administrators reconfigure servers. For example, files can be mistakenly deleted, renamed, or moved from the correct directory. If they are, links, graphics, and scripts will not work, especially if you used absolute path names.

Updates involve adding, deleting, or revising pages and links. You have to be certain that changes you make do not introduce any errors. Perform the tests you ran when first posting your pages (see page 102).

Update your files the same way you posted them to the server originally (see page 120). You can send them over the Internet if a few small files need updating. Be sure to arrange this with the system administrator.

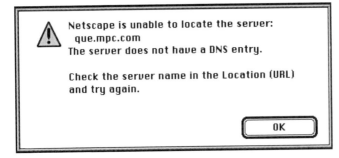

This message results from a bad server address in the URL.

Check-ups add a few items to the normal testing procedure conducted before you posted the files.

- Is your home page located at the correct URL?

- Are the linked pages, graphics, and gateway scripts at the correct URLs?

- Do links work?

- Do graphics load?

- Do gateway scripts run?

- Do forms send input to the correct gateway script?

- Do responses, if any, return to browsers from gateway scripts?

- Do you get the correctly processed data from gateway scripts?

- Are links to other peoples' documents still valid URLs?

- Is the information still current and relevant?

- Are pointer pages in place for files that moved to new URLs?

- Do searchable indexes have your pages listed in their databases?

- What do usage reports from the server tell you about your document?

- Did you address issues brought to your attention by users? Your home page should have your e-mail address in case users find something wrong.

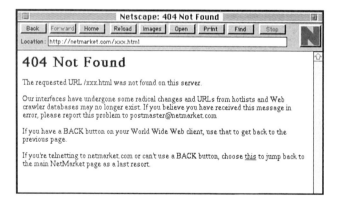

This message comes from a server that could not find the file you requested. The path or filename portion of the URL is incorrect.

How to Find Things on the Web

Automated search engines help you find things on the Web. Search engines are like the information booth at a mall; you tell the person at the booth what you are looking for, jewelry for example, and they give you a list of stores that may have what you need. They also show you where to find the stores in the mall.

All search engines work pretty much the same. You fill out a form that defines the search parameters and words you want to find, and the engine searches for URLs (file names), titles of documents, linked text, and URLs in linked text. When it completes the search, the results are displayed on your screen as links to the files that match your search criteria. You can then use the link to jump directly to the file.

Some search engines include many topics, others are limited to specific technical databases, individual journals, or libraries. Some searchable indexes are listed on the facing page. Some are slow but contain a wealth of information. Others are quick but less thorough. Find one that indexes the kind of information you are looking for. A search engine usually makes available an explanation of its content and method of compiling it.

Another way to find things on the Web is with the help of a directory. A directory is like the card catalog at a library or the table of contents in a book. You look through the lists of pages for one that interests you. Most of these are grouped into listings of related topics to help you find these by topics. The CERN W3 Servers, Yahoo, and EINet Galaxy pages list on the next page includes directories.

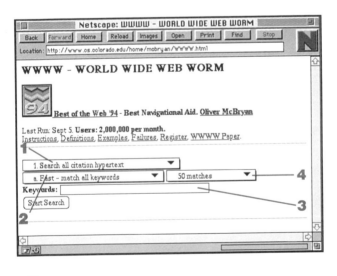

1. Choose part of the Web documents that you want the engine to search.

2. Choose one of the search methods.

3. Type the words you want to search for.

4. Choose the number of matches you want to see.

Some Web Indexes

Search Engine	URL
Aliweb	**http://web.nexor.co.uk/aliweb/doc/aliweb.html**
CERN W3 Servers	**http://info.cern.ch/hypertext/DataSources/WWW/Servers.html**
EINet Galaxy	**http://galaxy.einet.net/about.html**
Lycos	**http://http://lycos.cs.cmu.edu/**
WebCrawler	**http://www.biotech.washington.edu/ webcrawler/webcrawler.html**
World Wide Web Worm	**http://www.cs.colorado.edu/home/mcbryan/WWWW.html**
Yahoo	**http://www.yahoo.com/**

For a larger list of search engines and directories, see the W3 Search Engines page at **http://cuiwww.unige.ch/meta-index.html**.

The search engine returns the results as a list of links.

Getting Your Files Noticed

One way to get your files noticed by people browsing the Web is by listing them with searchable indexes (some of these indexes are listed on page 134). Find the ones that fit your audience: if your audience is wide, list files with a general interest index that includes many topics; if your readership is targeted, find an index limited to special interest areas.

You should check all indexes periodically for your files. Some indexes collect information automatically, others require you to submit your URLs to the database through a form. Conduct test searches that should result in matches to your files. Use words that other people would think of using, not the word you know results in a match. Remember, indexes search for URLs (file names), titles of documents, which are different from the file names, linked text, and URLs in linked text.

There are offline ways of getting noticed as well.

- Use traditional media for publicizing your files. People still read, listen to radio, and watch television news programs. Press releases can get you in those media.

- Advertise if you have the budget.

- Include the URL in the address block of any printed materials.

Some indexes ask for very basic information, which they use later to index your files automatically.

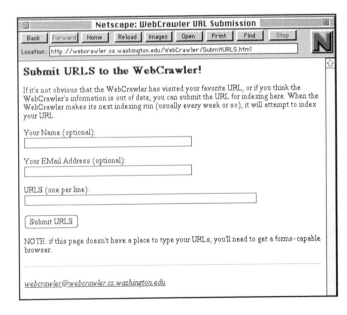

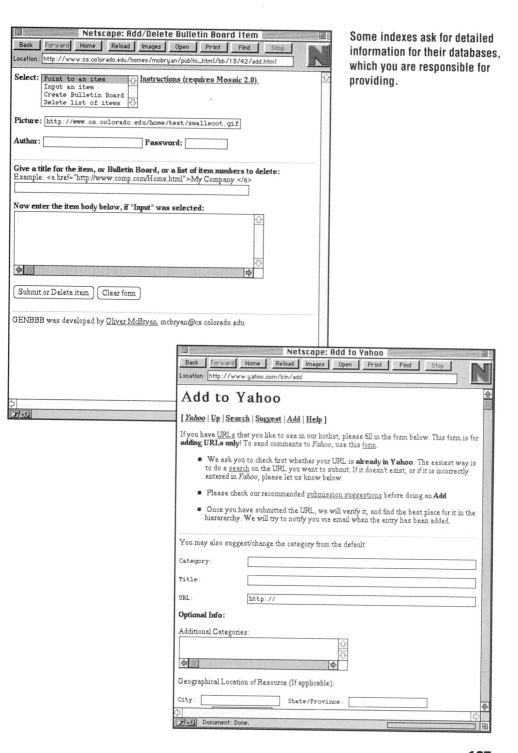

Some indexes ask for detailed information for their databases, which you are responsible for providing.

Naming Files and Links

There are at least two good reasons for using plain English when naming files, titles in headers, linked text, and URLs. First, you and those you work with won't need crib sheets to remember what's in the files. Second, and most important, people find your files through searchable indexes that catalog the names you choose.

People think of words to search for the way they talk. They tend to try whole words first, like Rottweiler, Abyssinian, and amortization rather than rtwlr, absinin, and amort. Use common words whenever possible.

Indexes also catalog the actual text used as the link. Use linked text that has meaning. Linking the words *click this* for more on heart attacks won't do you much good in a search index. But linking the words *heart attack* will.

A naming system helps you keep track of files and makes updates easier. Clever naming systems based on abbreviations and numbers mean nothing to people unfamiliar with your system. They are meaningless in an index and are unlikely to ever come up in a search.

Some servers place constraints on the number of characters in a file name. Use short words and common abbreviations for file names on these servers.

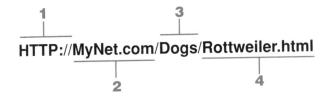

1 The HTTP:// in front of a URL indicates a Web site.

2 A domain has a suffix that indicates what kind of organization runs the Web site.

3 Use slashes to separate any directory names.

4 Put the HTML file name at the end.

The title in the head of an HTML file appears at the top of the browser window.

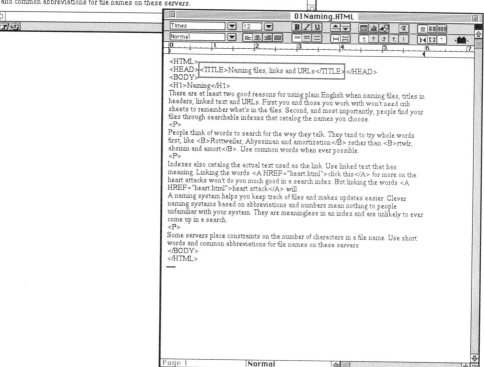

Where to Find Software on the Web

Much of the software that you will use with the Web is freeware (software that you don't have to pay for) and shareware (software that you can download and try for a limited time before paying for). You can find most of this software at popular anonymous FTP sites or via the Web, if you know where to look.

If you need Web browsers and HTML tools, here are some good places to look:

Windows Software

Description	URL
Mosaic and Viewers	ftp://ftp.ncsa.uiuc.edu/Web/Mosaic/Windows
HTML	ftp://ftp.ncsa.uiuc.edu/Web/html/Windows
Netscape	ftp://ftp.netscape.com/netscape/windows
W4 Server (Windows 3.1 and Win95)	http://130.89.232.242/
Windows httpd (Web Server)	http://www.city.net/win-httpd/
Freeware HTTP Server for Windows NT	ftp://emwac.ed.ac.uk/pub/https/

Macintosh Software

Description	URL
Mosaic and Viewers	ftp://ftp.ncsa.uiuc.edu/Web/Mosaic/Mac
HTML	ftp://ftp.ncsa.uiuc.edu/Web/html/Mac
HTML	ftp://ftp.hawaii.edu/mirrors/infomac/TextProcessing/HTML
Netscape	ftp://ftp.netscape.com/netscape/mac
MacHTTP (Web Server)	http://www.biap.com/machttp/machttp_software.html

UNIX Software

Description	URL
Mosaic and Viewers	ftp://ftp.ncsa.uiuc.edu/Web/Mosaic/Unix
Netscape	ftp://ftp.netscape.com/netscape/unix
HTML	ftp://ftp.ncsa.uiuc.edu/Web/html/hotmetal/SPARC-Motif
tkWWW (HTML and Web browser)	ftp://ftp.aud.alcatel.com/tcl/extensions/
NCSA httpd (Web Server)	http://hoohoo.ncsa.uiuc.edu/docs/setup/Download.html
CERN HTTP (Web Server)	http://www.w3.org/hypertext/WWW/Daemon/Status.html

If you need other types of software not directly related to the Web, check one of these other FTP sites with good collections:

Windows Software

Description	URL
Internet Software	ftp://ftp.cica.indiana.edu/pub/pc/win3/winsock
Microsoft	ftp://ftp.microsoft.com

Mac Software

Description	URL
Internet Software	ftp://ftp.hawaii.edu/mirrors/infomac/Communication/MacTCP
More Internet Software	ftp://mac.archive.umich.edu/mac/util/comm

UNIX Software

Description	URL
UNIX Software	ftp://ftp.uu.net/systems/unix
UNIX Software	ftp://sunsite.unc.edu/pub/packages
UNIX Software	ftp://wuarchive.wustl.edu/systems/unix
Linux Software	ftp://wuarchive.wustl.edu/systems/linux

Glossary

Absolute path Absolute paths spell out the location of a file by starting at the highest level and listing each directory needed to find the file itself.

AIFF A common sound file format on the Macintosh.

Anchor Text and graphics can link to places within the same document. These links require two parts: the anchor and the link. The anchor identifies the place to jump to.

Anonymous FTP FTP transactions that do not require a unique login name or password. Use the name *anonymous* to login and use your e-mail address as a password.

Argument Words or numbers you enter as part of an HTML tag to expand or modify how that tag operates.

ASCII Acronym for American Standard Code for Information Interchange, a standard character set.

Authoring software Computer programs that aid in creating HTML documents by inserting the code for tags.

Body HTML tag used to enclose the body (all the text and tags) of the HTML document.

Browser A program used to view HTML documents and navigate the World Wide Web. See *Netscape, Mosaic,* and *Lynx.*

Byte Eight bits; the fundamental unit of personal computer data.

CERN European Particle Physics Laboratory, the developers of the World Wide Web.

CGI (Common Gateway Interface) The scripting language used to write gateway scripts for CERN and NCSA Web servers.

Check boxes Used in forms to make it possible to select one or more non-exclusive options in a list.

Coordinates Pairs of numbers used to define the edges of the clickable areas in clickable image maps.

Default The initial value of any input type (text field, check box, radio button, selection list) used in a form.

Dedicated connection Access to the Internet that is always available via a special connection such as FDDI, T1, or switched 56. See *dial-up connections* and *ISDN.*

Dial-up connections Accessing the Internet by means of a modem and communication software.

Directory A major division on a hard drive or server used to divide and organize files.

Domain The name for a company, organization, or individual's Internet connection. Individual computers within this domain all end with the domain a part of their host name.

Download To transfer a file from another computer to your computer.

E-mail (electronic mail). A communication system that allows you to send an electronic "letter" to one or more recipients.

Ethernet A standard for local area network hardware, cabling, and transmission.

External files Any files that are not directly loadable by a browser such as some image formats, sounds, videos, or even program files.

FDDI (Fiber Distributed Data Interface) A type of high-speed dedicated connection to the Internet with a speed of 45 MB per second.

File formats The patterns and standards used to store a program on a disk. Examples are GIF, JPEG, AIFF.

142

Form A part of HTML documents designed with fill-in text boxes, lists of options, and other elements that allow the user of the form to send information back to the Web server.

Freeware Software that is distributed at no cost to the user. (the author maintains the copyright).

FTP (File Transfer Protocol) The standard method of transferring files from one computer to another via the Internet.

Gateway script A program that is run on a Web server that processes the input from forms.

GIF A popular type of image file format.

Gopher A menu-based information system on the Internet popularized because of its ability to interconnect different Gopher sites on the same menu.

Graphical browser A program used to view formatted HTML documents and navigate the World Wide Web. Graphical browsers can display inline images and display text in various type styles. Examples are Mosaic and Netscape.

Head The HTML tag used to enclose the beginning elements in the HTML document, including the title.

Home page The first HTML document that you intend people to see at your Web site is known as a home page.

Host name The name of a computer on the Internet, used to identify it in the URL naming scheme.

HTML (Hypertext Markup Language) The coding scheme used to format text for use on the World Wide Web.

HTTP (Hypertext Transport Protocol) The transmission standard used to send HTML documents across the World Wide Web.

Hypertext An interlinked document structure that allows you to jump freely from one topic or document to another.

Internet The general term used to describe the worldwide network of computers and services encompassing some 20–40 million computer users and dozens of information systems including e-mail, Gopher, FTP, and the World Wide Web.

Internet access fees Costs charged by Internet access providers to connect to the Internet.

Internet access provider A company that sells connections to the Internet to other companies and individuals. Also called *Internet service provider*.

ISDN (Integrated Digital Services Network) A high-speed dial-up connection to the Internet. Availability and cost are determined in part by local telephone companies.

LAN (Local Area Network) A group of computers within one office or department that typically share printers, servers, and the ability to send e-mail within the group.

Linear document A type of organization for HTML documents in which one HTML file follows the next. The HTML author determines the order in which the information is presented.

Link The text or graphic used in an HTML document to jump from one document to another.

Load time The amount of time it takes a user to retrieve a Web page and view it in a browser on their computer.

Localtalk A local area network standard used by Macintosh computers.

Lynx A non-graphical browser for UNIX and DOS systems. See also *Netscape* and *Mosaic*.

Macintosh A brand of personal computers manufactured by Apple Computer.

Menu An on-screen display that lists available choices.

Method The manner in which an HTML form is submitted to the Web server. The most common method is *post*.

Modem A device that converts digital information from a computer to analog information that can be sent over telephone lines. This allows computers equipped with modems to communicate over telephone lines.

Monospaced font A typeface in which the width of each character is the same.

Mosaic One of the first graphical browsers. Developed by the NCSA, this browser fueled the growth of the Web. It is available in versions for Windows, Mac, and UNIX.

MPEG (Motion Picture Experts Group) A standard and file format for motion video on computers.

Multimedia Documents that combine text, graphics, sound, movies, or other media.

Named entity Special characters whose HTML code is an ampersand (&) followed by a name.

NCSA (National Center for Supercomputing Applications) The research group that developed Mosaic, a popular graphical browser.

Netscape A popular commercial graphical browser. It is available in versions for Windows, Mac, and UNIX.

Network administrator The person responsible for maintaining a network and assisting its users.

Non-graphical browser A program used to view HTML documents and navigate the World Wide Web. Non-graphical browsers do not display inline images and do not display formatted text. An example is Lynx.

Non-linear document A type of organization for HTML documents in which one HTML file contains links to more than one other HTML file. The person browsing the files determines the order in which the information is presented.

Numbered entity Special characters whose HTML code is an ampersand (&) followed by a number.

Operating system A master control program for a computer. Examples are DOS, UNIX, and the MacOS. (Technically speaking, Microsoft Windows 3.x is an operating environment as it still requires the separate DOS operating system to run. Microsoft's Windows95 is a true operating system as DOS is built-in to it.)

Path name The place where a file is stored on a computer, indicated by the drive or volume name and the subdirectories needed to find the file. See *relative path* and *absolute path*.

Platform A computer hardware standard, such as IBM PC compatible or Macintosh.

Post To place an HTML file on a Web server to make it available for browsing.

Preference setting Program options in browsers that allow the user to determine such things as which fonts are used for various HTML styles, whether or not inline images are displayed, what other applications are used to view movies, and so on.

Proportional font A typeface in which the width of each character varies depending on the character's shape. An *I* takes up less space than *w* for example.

Public domain software Software that is made freely available by the developer and which the developer gives up all copyright ownership to.

Radio button Used in forms to make it possible to select one exclusive option in a list.

RAM (Random Access Memory) The computer's primary working memory in which program instructions and data are stored.

Relative path Relative paths spell out the location of a file based on the current document location.

Router A device connecting a LAN to the Internet that routes transmissions between the two.

Searchable Index Indexes of World Wide Web documents that you can submit a query to and the index will search to find pages matching your specification.

Server See *Web server.*

Shareware Software that you can obtain for free (often by downloading from the Internet) on a trial basis but that may require some payment or registration for continued use.

Sound card Hardware used to play sound files on computers.

Submit To send a completed form to a Web server.

T1 A high-speed dedicated connection to the Internet that provides data transmission rates of 1.5 MB per second.

Tag The HTML codes used to specify text styles, links, graphics, and other HTML elements.

Text fields Form elements that allow users to insert a single line of text.

Title The HTML tag used to give each HTML document a title.

Transmission line The physical connection from your computer to the Internet such as a telephone line or a T1.

Transparent graphics Graphic images that have a clear background, which makes the graphic appear to float in the browser screen.

UNIX An operating system used on a variety of computers from personal computers to mainframe. Many computers and servers connected to the Internet use UNIX.

URL (Uniform Resource Locator) The standard used to identify files on the Internet and World Wide Web using the type of server, the host name of the computer the file is on, and the complete path to the file.

Video player Hardware used to play movie files on computers, such as QuickTime.

WAV A popular sound file format used primarily by Windows-based computers.

Web server The hardware and software used to store and deliver HTML documents for use on the World Wide Web.

Web site A person or company's collection of HTML documents on a Web server. A single Web server may contain one or more Web sites.

Windows An operating environment for the IBM PC-compatible platform that allows several programs to run at once and utilizes icons and menus for program control.

Word processor A program used to create and edit text documents. When using a word processor to create HTML documents, save the documents as ASCII text rather than in the word processor's proprietary format.

World Wide Web (WWW) An Internet service that links multimedia documents together using hypertext. Users can jump between documents using links to view text, graphics, movies, and other media.

ASCII Codes

Decimal	Name	Character	Decimal	Name	Character
0	blank		31	down triangle	▼
1	happy face	☺	32	space	Space
2	inverse happy face	●	33	exclamation point	!
3	heart	♥	34	quotation mark	"
4	diamond	♦	35	number sign	#
5	club	♣	36	dollar sign	$
6	spade	♠	37	percent sign	%
7	bullet	•	38	ampersand	&
8	inverse bullet	◙	39	apostrophe	'
9	circle	o	40	opening parenthesis	(
10	inverse circle	◙	41	closing parenthesis	)
11	male sign	♂	42	asterisk	*
12	female sign	♀	43	plus sign	+
13	single note	♪	44	comma	,
14	double note	♫	45	hyphen or minus sign	-
15	sun	☼	46	period	.
16	right triangle	►	47	slash	/
17	left triangle	◄	48	zero	0
18	up/down arrow	↕	49	one	1
19	double exclamation	‼	50	two	2
20	paragraph sign	¶	51	three	3
21	section sign	§	52	four	4
22	rectangular bullet	■	53	five	5
23	up/down to line	↨	54	six	6
24	up arrow	↑	55	seven	7
25	down arrow	↓	56	eight	8
26	right arrow	→	57	nine	9
27	left arrow	←	58	colon	:
28	lower left box	∟	59	semicolon	;
29	left/right arrow	↔	60	less-than sign	<
30	up triangle	▲			

Decimal	Name	Character	Decimal	Name	Character
61	equal sign	=	97	lowercase A	a
62	greater-than sign	>	98	lowercase B	b
63	question mark	?	99	lowercase C	c
64	at sign	@	100	lowercase D	d
65	capital A	A	101	lowercase E	e
66	capital B	B	102	lowercase F	f
67	capital C	C	103	lowercase G	g
68	capital D	D	104	lowercase H	h
69	capital E	E	105	lowercase I	i
70	capital F	F	106	lowercase J	j
71	capital G	G	107	lowercase K	k
72	capital H	H	108	lowercase L	l
73	capital I	I	109	lowercase M	m
74	capital J	J	110	lowercase N	n
75	capital K	K	111	lowercase O	o
76	capital L	L	112	lowercase P	p
77	capital M	M	113	lowercase Q	q
78	capital N	N	114	lowercase R	r
79	capital O	O	115	lowercase S	s
80	capital P	P	116	lowercase T	t
81	capital Q	Q	117	lowercase U	u
82	capital R	R	118	lowercase V	v
83	capital S	S	119	lowercase W	w
84	capital T	T	120	lowercase X	x
85	capital U	U	121	lowercase Y	y
86	capital V	V	122	lowercase Z	z
87	capital W	W	123	opening brace	{
88	capital X	X	124	vertical line	|
89	capital Y	Y	125	closing brace	}
90	capital Z	Z	126	tilde	~
91	opening bracket	[	127	small house	🏠
92	backward slash	\	128	C cedilla	Ç
93	closing bracket	]	129	u umlaut	ü
94	caret	^	130	e acute	é
95	underscore	_	131	a circumflex	â
96	grave	`			

(continues)

Decimal	Name	Character	Decimal	Name	Character
132	a umlaut	ä	168	opening question mark	¿
133	a grave	à	169	upper left box	⌐
134	a ring	å	170	upper right box	¬
135	c cedilla	ç	171	1/2	$\frac{1}{2}$
136	e circumflex	ê	172	1/4	$\frac{1}{4}$
137	e umlaut	ë	173	opening exclamation	¡
138	e grave	è	174	opening guillemets	«
139	I umlaut	Ï	175	closing guillemets	»
140	I circumflex	Î	176	light block	░
141	I grave	Ì	177	medium block	▒
142	A umlaut	Ä	178	dark block	▓
143	A ring	Å	179	single vertical	│
144	E acute	É	180	single right junction	┤
145	ae ligature	æ	181	2 to 1 right junction	╡
146	AE ligature	Æ	182	1 to 2 right junction	╢
147	o circumflex	ô	183	1 to 2 upper right	╖
148	o umlaut	ö	184	2 to 1 upper right	╕
149	o grave	ò	185	double right junction	╣
150	u circumflex	û	186	double vertical	║
151	u grave	ù	187	double upper right	╗
152	y umlaut	ÿ	188	double lower right	╝
153	O umlaut	Ö	189	1 to 2 lower right	╜
154	U umlaut	Ü	190	2 to 1 lower right	╛
155	cent sign	¢	191	single upper right	┐
156	pound sign	£	192	single lower left	└
157	yen sign	¥	193	single lower junction	┴
158	Pt	₧	194	single upper junction	┬
159	function	ƒ	195	single left junction	├
160	a acute	á	196	single horizontal	─
161	I acute	í	197	single intersection	┼
162	o acute	ó			
163	u acute	ú			
164	n tilde	ñ			
165	N tilde	Ñ			
166	a macron	a̱			
167	o macron	o̱			

Decimal	Name	Character	Decimal	Name	Character
198	2 to 1 left junction	╞	229	sigma	σ
199	1 to 2 left junction	╟	230	mu	μ
200	double lower left	╚	231	tau	τ
201	double upper left	╔	232	Phi	Φ
202	double lower junction	╩	233	theta	θ
203	double upper junction	╦	234	Omega	Ω
204	double left junction	╠	235	delta	δ
205	double horizontal	═	236	infinity	∞
206	double intersection	╬	237	phi	σ
207	1 to 2 lower junction	╧	238	epsilon	ε
208	2 to 1 lower junction	╨	239	intersection of sets	∩
209	1 to 2 upper junction	╤	240	is identical to	≡
210	2 to 1 upper junction	╥	241	plus/minus sign	±
211	1 to 2 lower left	╙	242	greater/equal sign	≥
212	2 to 1 lower left	╘	243	less/equal sign	≤
213	2 to 1 upper left	╒	244	top half integral	⌠
214	1 to 2 upper left	╓	245	lower half integral	⌡
215	2 to 1 intersection	╫	246	divide-by sign	÷
216	1 to 2 intersection	╪	247	approximately	≈
217	single lower right	┘	248	degree	°
218	single upper right	┌	249	filled-in degree	°
219	inverse space	█	250	small bullet	·
220	lower inverse	▄	251	square root	√
221	left inverse	▌	252	superscript n	n
222	right inverse	▐	253	superscript 2	2
223	upper inverse	▀	254	box	■
224	alpha	α	255	phantom space	
225	beta	β			
226	Gamma	Γ			
227	pi	π			
228	Sigma	Σ			

HTML Code by Type

Tag Name	Code	Page
Document Structure		
Body	<BODY>	28
Head	<HEAD>	28
HTML	<HTML>	28
Titles and Headings		
Heading - First Level	<H1>	28
Heading - Second Level	<H2>	28
Heading - Third Level	<H3>	28
Heading - Fourth Level	<H4>	28
Heading - Fifth Level	<H5>	28
Heading - Sixth Level	<H6>	28
Title	<Title>	28
Paragraphs and Lines		
Break	 	34
Horizontal Rule	<HR>	50
Paragraph	<P>	28
Links		
Anchor	<A NAME="*name*">	44
Link	<A>	16
Link to an anchor	<A NAME="*anchor name*">	16
Link to another document	<A HREF="*filename*">	40
Linked graphic	<A HREF="*link filename*">	38
	<IMG SRC="*graphic filename*">	38
Linked text	<A HREF="*link filename*">*text to click*</A>	36
Character Formats		
Address	<ADDRESS>	30
Blockquote	<BLOCKQUOTE>	48
Bold	<B>	32
Code Sample	<CODE>	30
Emphasis	<EM>	30
Italic	<I>	32
Keyboard	<KBD>	30
Preformatted Type	<PRE>	64

150

Tag Name	Code	Page
Character Formats		
Strong	<STRONG>	30
Typewriter	<TT>	32
Underscore	<U>	32
Graphics		
Alternate to Image	<ALT>	42
Image Alignment	<IMG ALIGN=*[top, middle, bottom]* SRC="*filename*">	54
Images	<IMG SRC="*filename*"	52
Image map	<IMG SRC="*image filename*" ISMAP>	68
Lists		
Ordered List	<OL>	58
Unordered List	<UL>	58
List Item	<LI>	58
Glossary Lists	<DL>	60
Definition Lists	See Glossary Lists	60
Glossary List Terms	<DT>	60
Glossary List Definitions	<DD>	60
Forms		
Form	<FORM>	74
Submit button	<input type=submit value="Submit">	74
Reset button	<input type=reset value="Clear">	74
Text Field	<input type="text" size="*xx*" name="*name*" maxlength="*yy*" value="*default*">	76
Radio button	<input type="radio" name="*name*" value="value"*[checked]*>	78
Check box	<input type="checkbox" name="*name*" value="*value*" *[checked]*>	80
Popup list name	<select name="*name*">	82
Selection List	See *Popup List name*	82
Popup list option	<option>	82
Popup list selected option	<option selected>	82
Other Tags		
Comment	<!-*comment*->	98
Special Characters	&*character code*;	62

Alphabetical Listing of HTML Code

Tag Name	Code	Page
Address	<ADDRESS>	30
Alternate to Image	<ALT>	42
Anchor	<A NAME="*name*">	44
Blockquote	<BLOCKQUOTE>	48
Body	<BODY>	28
Bold	<B>	32
Break	 	34
Check box	<input type="checkbox" name="*name*" value="*value*" [checked]>	80
Code Sample	<CODE>	30
Comment	<!-*comment*->	98
Definition Lists	See Glossary Lists	60
Emphasis	<EM>	30
Form	<FORM>	74
Glossary Lists	<DL>	60
Glossary List Definitions	<DD>	60
Glossary List Terms	<DT>	60
Head	<HEAD>	28
Heading - First Level	<H1>	28
Heading - Second Level	<H2>	28
Heading - Third Level	<H3>	28
Heading - Fourth Level	<H4>	28
Heading - Fifth Level	<H5>	28
Heading - Sixth Level	<H6>	28
Horizontal Rule	<HR>	50
HTML	<HTML>	28
Image Alignment	<IMG ALIGN=*[top, middle, bottom]* SRC="*filename*">	54
Image map	<IMG SRC="*image filename*" ISMAP>	68
Images	<IMG SRC="*filename*">	52
Italic	<I>	32
Keyboard	<KBD>	30
Link	<A HREF="*filename*">	40
Linked graphic	<A HREF="*link filename*">	38

Tag Name	Code	Page
	<IMG SRC="*graphic filename*">	38
Linked text	<A HREF="*link filename*"> *text to click*</A>	36
List Item	<LI>	58
Ordered List	<OL>	58
Paragraph	<P>	28
Popup list selected option	<option selected>	82
Popup list name	<select name="*name*">	82
Popup list option	<option>	82
Preformatted Type	<PRE>	64
Radio button	<input type="radio" name="*name*" value="value"*[checked]*>	78
Reset button	<input type=reset value="Clear">	74
Selection List	See *Popup List name*	82
Special Characters	&*character code*;	62
Strong	<STRONG>	30
Submit button	<input type=submit value="Submit">	74
Text Field	<input type="text" size="*xx*" name="*name*" maxlength="*yy*" value="*default*">	76
Title	<Title>	28
Typewriter	<TT>	32
Underscore	<U>	32
Unordered List	<UL>	58

Index

Symbols

A

B

C

G

gateway scripts, 15, 143
  forms, 72-75
  image maps, 68-69
GIF Converter, 56-57
GIF graphics, converting, 56-57, 143
glossary lists, 60-61
Gopher sites, 41, 143
government (Web servers), 123
graphical browsers, 18, 144
graphics, 17
  alignment, 54-55
  converting formats, 56-57
  display
    browser interpretation, 95
    non-graphical browsers, 19, 42-43
    graphical browsers, 18
  image maps, 68-69, 142
  inserting in documents, 52-53
  links, 38-39, 44-45
  rules, 50-51
  transfer times, 53, 95, 144
    notes about file sizes, 96
    testing, 102
Great Lakes Area Commercial Internet, 128

H

hardware requirements, 22-24
  browsers, 25
  sound, 24
  video, 24
  Web servers, 126-12
Harvard Smithsonian Center for Astrophysics home page, 85
head (documents), 28, 144
headings, 28
  document navigation, 92-93
  styles, 30-31
helper applications, 16

Hewlett Packard home page, 21
home pages, 84, 144
  advertising, 136-137
  body, 28
  check-ups, 132-133
  creating, 28
  design issues, 94-95
  graphics, 17
  head, 28
  linear design, 23, 86-87, 90, 144
  links
    within the same document, 44-45
    what's new links, 96
  multimedia, 145
  naming, 138-139
  navigation methods
    bottom-of-file options, 93
    headings, 92-93
    links, 91
    page numbers, 92-93
    table of contents, 90
    top-of-file options, 93
  non-linear design, 23, 88-89, 145
  posting, 120-121, 146
  proofreading, 102
  search tools
    indexes, 21
  separator rules, 50-51
  sound, 17
  table of contents, 85
  testing, 102-103
  updating, 132-133
  text, *see* text
Home Pages Inc., 128
horizontal rules, 50-51
host names, 144
HoTMetaL
  UNIX, 108-109
  Windows, 116-117
HTML Assistant 118-119
HTML.Edit for the Macintosh, 106-107
HTML Editor 1.0 for the Macintosh, 104-105
HTML files, *see* documents

html-helper-mode, 110-111
HTML software, 140-141
HTTP (HyperText Transport Protocol), 144
HTTP Server for Windows NT, 140
hypertext, 13, 16, 144
  anchors (links), 44-45
  creating links, 36-37
  naming links, 138-139
  navigation by links, 91
  what's new links, 96

I

image maps, 68-69, 142
indexes (World Wide Web), 21, 134-137, 146
inline graphics
  alignment, 54-55
  display
    browser interpretation, 95
    non-graphical browsers, 19, 42-43
    graphical browsers, 18
  image maps, 68-69, 142
  links, 38-39
    anchors, 44-45
  transfer times, 53, 95, 144
    notes about file sizes, 96
    testing, 102
  see also graphics
input (forms), 74-75
  check boxes, 80-81
  passwords, 76-77
  radio buttons, 78-79
  selection lists, 82-83
  text fields, 76-77, 147
Internet, 15, 143-144
  connections, 26-27
  host names, 144
  service providers, 14, 127-129, 144
Internet Assistant, 112-113
Internet Distribution Services, 128
Internet Information Services Inc., 128

numbered entities, 62-63,
145
numbered lists, 58-59

O

opaque graphics,
converting to transparent
graphics, 56-57, 147
opening tags, 28
operating systems, 146
ordered lists, 58-59

P

page numbers
(documents), 92-93
paragraphs, 28-29, 34-35
passwords (forms), 76-77
paths (URLs), 17, 46-47,
145
phone numbers, 30
The Pipeline, 129, 131
platforms (browsers), 19,
146
pop-up menus (forms),
82-83
postal addresses, 30
posting documents,
120-121, 146
preferences (browsers),
see display preferences
(browsers)
preformatted text, 64-65
Primenet, 129
proportional fonts, 146
programming
comments, 98-99
formatting code, 100-101
testing code, 102-103
proofreading documents,
102
PSINet, 129
public domain software,
20, 146

Q

QuakeNet, 129
Quantum Networking
Solutions, 129

QuickTime video files,
66-67
quotes (block quotes),
48-49

R

radio buttons (forms),
78-79, 146
RAM (random access
memory), 146
relative paths (URLs),
46-47
relative tags, 30
research institutions
(World Wide Web), 21,
122
reserved characters, 62-63
restricted access notes, 96
routers, 126, 146
rules, 50-51

S

sample text, 30-31
scripts (gateway scripts), 15
forms, 72-75
image maps, 68-69
scrolling lists (forms),
82-83
Scrolls from the Dead Sea
home page, 123
The SEAMLESS WEBSite,
129
searches
forms, 71
World Wide Web, 21,
134-137, 146
security of financial
transactions, 20
separator rules, 50-51
servers, see Web servers
service providers
(Internet), 14, 127-129,
144
shareware, 140-141, 146
shopping (World Wide
Web), 20
slash (/) closing tags, 28
The Sphere, 129

SoftQuad (HoTMetaL),
108-109, 116-117
software
requirements, 22, 24
browsers, 25
sound, 24
video, 24
Web sites, 140-141
sound, 17
hardware requirements,
24
links, 66-67
notes about file sizes, 96
software requirements, 24
sound cards, 147
transfer time, 66-67, 102
special characters, 62-63
speed (Internet connec-
tions), 26-27
spell checking documents,
102
SSNet, 129
Stelcom, 129
Streams Online Media
Development, 129
strong text, 30-31
styles (text)
addresses, 30
computer code, 30-31
emphasis, 30-31
headings, 30-31
keyboard, 30-31
sample, 30-31
strong, 30-31
submission of forms,
72-75, 147
symbols, 62-63
system administrators
(Web servers), 127, 145

T

T1 dedicated connections
(Internet), 26, 147
T3 dedicated connections
(Internet), 26
table of contents
(home pages), 85, 90